KU-067-732

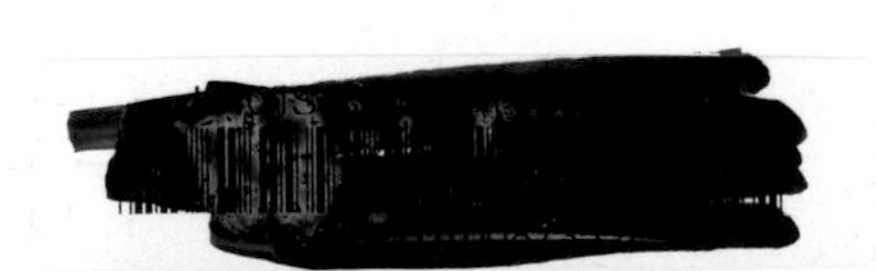

The Bridgestone
100 Best Restaurants in Ireland

2011 EDITION

www.bridgestoneguides.com

THE BRIDGESTONE

100 BEST RESTAURANTS IN IRELAND 2011

JOHN McKENNA - SALLY McKENNA

ESTRAGON PRESS

FIRST PUBLISHED IN JANUARY 2011

BY ESTRAGON PRESS

DURRUS

COUNTY CORK

ISBN -978-1-906927-06-6

TYPESET IN GILL ALTERNATE TO

AN ORIGINAL DESIGN BY NICK CANN

ILLUSTRATIONS BY AOIFE WASSER

PRINTED IN SPAIN BY GRAPHYCEMS

• Front cover photos courtesy: Top left, Inis Meáin Restaurant & Suites. Top Right, O'Brien's Chop House. Middle left, Gregan's Castle. Middle right, Pearl Brasserie. Bottom left, Gregan's Castle. Bottom right, The Oarsman.

WRITTEN & EDITED BY JOHN McKENNA

CONTRIBUTING EDITORS:

EAMON BARRETT

ORLA BRODERICK

CAROLINE BYRNE

SABRINA CONNEELY

ELIZABETH FIELD

CLAIRE GOODWILLIE

CAROLINE HENNESSY

VALERIE O'CONNOR

JAKKI OWENS

LESLIE WILLIAMS

PUBLISHING EDITOR: SALLY McKENNA

EDITOR: JUDITH CASEY

EDITORIAL ASSISTANT & WEB PICTURE EDITOR: EVE CLANCY

WEB: FLUIDEDGE.IE

FOR:

Clara McGowan

WITH SPECIAL THANKS TO

Des Collins, Colm Conyngham, Pat Curran, Grainne Byrne, Julie Barrett, George Lane, Frank McKevitt, Margaret Deverell, Lelia McKenna, Miguel Sancho, Hugh Stancliffe, Eugene McSweeney, John Ward, Connie McKenna, Sam McKenna, PJ McKenna and all our colleagues at Gill & Macmillan.

Bridgestone is the world's largest tyre and rubber company.

• Founded in Japan in 1931, it currently employs over 100,000 people in Europe, Asia and America and its products are sold in more than 150 countries. Its European plants are situated in France, Spain, Italy, Poland and Turkey.

• Bridgestone manufacture tyres for a wide variety of vehicles from passenger cars and motorcycles, trucks and buses to giant earthmovers and aircraft.

• Many new cars are fitted with Bridgestone tyres during manufacture, including Ford, Toyota, Volkswagen, Mercedes and BMW. Super cars such as Ferrari, Aston Martin and Porsche are also fitted with Bridgestone performance tyres as original equipment.

• Bridgestone commercial vehicle tyres enjoy a worldwide reputation for durability and its aircraft tyres are used by more than 100 airlines.

• In Formula 1 Bridgestone are sole tyre supplier with all the teams now competing on its Potenza racing tyres. Technology developed in the sport has led to increased performance and safety in Bridgestone's road tyres.

• Bridgestone tyres are distributed in Ireland by Bridgestone Ireland Ltd, a subsidiary of the multinational Bridgestone Corporation. A wide range of tyres is stocked in its 6,500 square metre central warehouse and its staff provide sales, technical and delivery services all over Ireland.

• Bridgestone tyres are available from First Stop Tyre Centres and tyre dealers throughout Ireland.

For further information:

BRIDGESTONE IRELAND LTD
10 Fingal Bay Business Park
Balbriggan
County Dublin

Tel: + 353 1 841 0000
Fax: + 353 1 841 5245

websites:
www.bridgestone.ie
www.firststop.ie
www.truckpoint.ie

• It is a story of success, and it is bewildering. Many of the restaurants featured in this book, and many of their counterparts in the 2011 edition of the *Bridgestone 100 Best Places to Stay*, have enjoyed a year of fabulous success.

• From Malin to Mizen, we have heard many, many stories of restaurants enjoying turnover that has gone up by 20%, and even 30%. And the success stories aren't confined to the best-known restaurants, who you might expect to weather the worst recession in Ireland's recent history better than newcomers and others.

• No, the rule that has emerged over the last year is simply this: if you are good, and you offer value and service and a signature style, then they will come. Never mind that other treats have gone by the board in these hard times: the Irish have chosen to continue to keep eating in good restaurants.

• But what has changed is the way in which they choose a place to eat. Today, the solid senders are the places that are flourishing, destinations that offer certainty in terms of quality and satisfaction, destinations with hard-won reputations, like Fishy Fishy in Kinsale, or Out Of The Blue in Dingle, or Dublin's Chapter One, or Harry's Bar in Inishowen.

• We applaud this smart behaviour by Ireland's food lovers. Quality should always win its just reward. The success stories may be somewhat bewildering, but they are a sign of the maturity of our food culture.

John & Sally McKenna
Durrus, West Cork, December 2010

"Throughout the world sounds one long cry from the heart of the artist: 'Give me the chance to do my very best'".

• This is what the cook Babette says, in Gabriel Axel's classic movie, *Babette's Feast.* It is also what every emerging chef says every day they walk into the kitchen and commence service, and it is one of the things we listen for when researching the annual *Bridgestone 100 Best Restaurants in Ireland.*

• Basically, we want the food to speak to us, and we want it to say: "Give me the chance to do my very best". We hope that inclusion in the 100 Best Restaurants is the critical equivalent of giving the new cook their chance: their chance to be heard, to be recognised, their chance to shine, the chance to do their best.

• Of course, there is a downside to this wish. When new talent emerges and emerges into these pages, others must move aside to make the space in this centurion of talent. This is not a criticism of the previous holders, simply a recognition of the fact that new talent must – must – be allowed its space.

• We hope that our desire to answer the "long cry from the heart of the artist" illuminates this choice of restaurants from all around Ireland. Babette gave of everything in preparing the feast for her guests. That is what artists do.

hot

Ananda Restaurant 49
Balloo House 123
The Ballymore Inn 87
Bon Appetit 50
Café Paradiso 32
Campagne 90
Chapter One 51
Cliff House Hotel 108
L'Ecrivain 53
Fishy Fishy Cafe 36
Ginger 126
Good Things Café 37
Gregan's Castle 26
Harry's Bar & Restaurant 47
Inis Meáin Restaurant & Suites 78
James Street South 127
Kappa-Ya 80
Knockranny House 100
MacNean Restaurant 23
Mourne Seafood Bar 128
The Old Convent 106
Out Of The Blue 85
Pichet 69
Rasam 72
Shu 130
The Tannery Restaurant 111
Thornton's 75
The Winding Stair 76

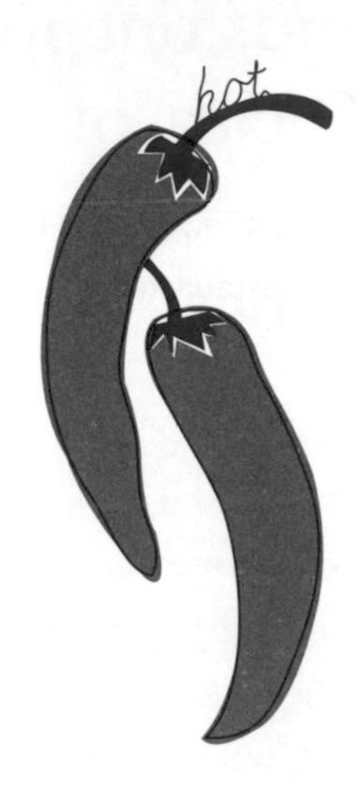

classic

Alden's 122
Ballymaloe House 31
Bassett's At Woodstock 89
Brocka on the Water 104
Café Hans 105

new

• The Bridgestone 100 Best Restaurants in Ireland is arranged alphabetically, by county, so it begins with County Carlow, which is followed by County Cavan, and so on. Within the counties, the entries are once again listed alphabetically. Entries in Northern Ireland are itemised alphabetically, at the end of the book. All NI prices are quoted in sterling.

• The contents of the Bridgestone 100 Best Guides are exclusively the result of the authors' deliberations. All meals and accommodation were paid for and any offers of discounts or gifts were refused.

• Many of the places featured in this book are only open during the summer, which means that they can be closed for any given length of time between October and March.

• **PRICES:** Dinner prices are calculated for an average three-course menu, without wine. Where the restaurant operates a set menu, that price is given.

• **LISTINGS:** In every entry in the book we try to list address, telephone number, and internet details. We also request details of disabled access, plus any other relevant information.

• **GPS CO-ORDINATES:** We have printed co-ordinates as provided to us by the various establishments, written in Decimal Degrees Format. The *Bridgestone Guides*, however, can accept no responsibility for the ultimate accuracy of the co-ordinates provided to us.

• **TELEPHONE NUMBERS:** Telephone numbers are listed using the international dialling code. If you are calling a number within the country, omit the international code and use the 0.

• **BRIDGESTONE PLAQUES:** Look out for the current year of our Bridgestone Plaques, displayed by many of our listed establishments.

SHA ROE BISTRO

Henry Stone & Stephanie Barrilier
Main Street, Clonegal
County Carlow
+353 (0) 53-937 5636
sha-roebistro@hotmail.com

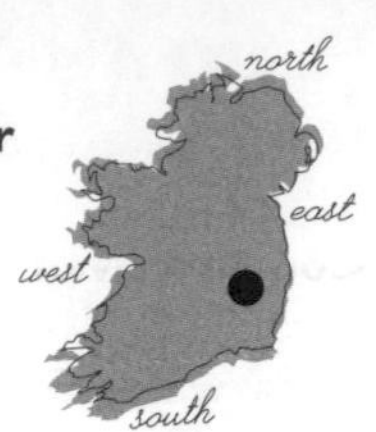

Intelligent planning and rigorous discipline means that Sha Roe never puts a foot wrong, and the comfort of the lovely old house is quite magical.

There is something in the aesthetic and the style of Sha Roe Bistro that charms the ladies. "It's great", says Claire Goodwillie of the Bridgestone parish. "Every mouthful was a pleasure", says Caroline Hennessy of the Bridgestone parish. What might explain this knack of charming the girls is the perfect integration of the design aesthetic in Sha Roe – it's the daintiest building in little Clonegal, and assuredly comfortable and quietly chic – with the culinary aesthetic they have practised here ever since opening back in 2006. Henry Stone lets his food talk for itself, but he knows how to make every plate count, so menus are kept very short, local foods are featured, and then the chef brings his flourish to the dishes, having already made sure that he's onto a good thing. He cooks fish beautifully, loves the unctuous nature of pork belly or a proper butternut squash risotto or a good pheasant and apple burger, and vegetables are always treated with care and concern. It's simple cooking, but wonderfully consistent, artistic and pleasing, and if you can nab the chef's table, go for it!

- **OPEN:** 7pm-9.30pm Wed-Sat; 12.30pm-3pm Sun
- **PRICE:** Sun Lunch €34, Dinner €40-€55
- **CREDIT CARDS:** Visa, Mastercard, Laser

● NOTES:
Wheelchair access with assistance.

● DIRECTIONS:
Just off the N80 Enniscorthy-Carlow road, 8km from Bunclody. From Wexford take the Enniscorthy-Bunclody road. From Kilkenny take the N10.

MacNEAN RESTAURANT

Neven & Amelda Maguire
Blacklion
County Cavan
+353 (0) 71-985 3022
www.macneanrestaurant.com
info@macneanrestaurant.com

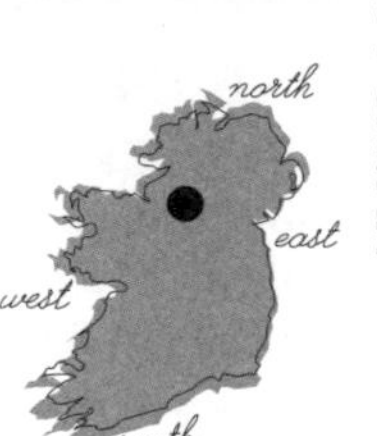

Walking down the road to Blacklion, with dinner at the MacNean as the evening's promise. What expectation!

The entire McKenna tribe decamped to Blacklion to enjoy a pair of dinners at the MacNean restaurant during the early summer of 2010. Of course, all the rooms were full, so we stayed down the road in a smart wee house, and walked down to the restaurant at night. Is there a greater sense of anticipation than to be walking down the road to Blacklion, with dinner cooked by Neven Maguire awaiting you? We don't think so. And was the expectation fulfilled? And how! Mr Maguire and his wife, Amelda, run a mighty machine in this little hamlet, and their staff back them to the hilt in offering stunning food: poached oyster with carrot ribbons; ravioli of crab in Thai broth; turbot with smoked pork belly and cep velouté; Irish beef including braised blade; sautéed fillet and beef cheek pie; Cashel Blue puff pizza with glazed pear; the incredible themed desserts to grandstand the conclusion of dinner. The restaurant is warm, sexy and fun, every single dish was magic, the energy of the enterprise courses through every single vein. Magic.

- **OPEN:** 6pm-9.30pm Wed-Sat, 7pm-8.30pm Sun; 12.30pm & 3.30pm Sun (closed Wed low season). Closed Jan
- **PRICE:** Sun Lunch €39, Dinner €70, Prestige €85
- **CREDIT CARDS:** Visa, Mastercard, Laser

- **NOTES:** Wheelchair access. Recommended for vegetarians, special menu. Ten guest rooms.

- **DIRECTIONS:**

On the main street in Blacklion, on the Sligo-Belfast road. GPS 54.291361 -7.877739

THE OLDE POST INN

Tara McCann & Gearoid Lynch
Cloverhill, Butler's Bridge
County Cavan
+353 (0) 47-55555
www.theoldepostinn.com
gearoidlynch@eircom.net

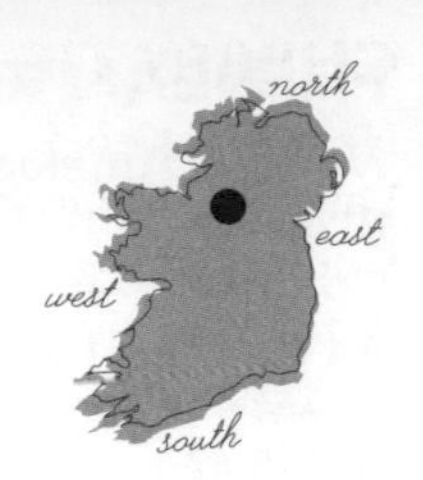

Gearoid Lynch has the technique of a great cook, but he isn't afraid to let his instinct temper that technique, and the two make for exciting, true cooking.

The great thing about Gearoid Lynch's cooking is that whilst he offers many of the standard repertoire dishes that characterise modern European cooking – bacon and cabbage terrine; prawns in ketaffi pastry; foie gras terrine; sirloin with bearnaise; suckling pig with poitin sauce; venison with Valrhona sauce – he cooks these dishes in a way which is entirely free of cliché. We have often mentioned how masterly he is at manipulating the textures of his dishes, and how this gives them a tactility that few other chefs can manage, But in fact he also brings an instinctual approach to his work, so no matter how obvious or venerable the dish – goat's cheese with beetroot; carpaccio of beef; Coq Hardi chicken – Mr Lynch's interpretation always seems freshly minted, newly thought-through, just out of the oven. It makes for great eating, eating that gives great pleasure and satisfaction, eating that make sense. And that satisfaction is copper-fastened by the warmth and comfort of the restaurant, the fantastic staff, and the cosy rooms that invite you to linger in lovely Cavan.

- **OPEN:** 6pm-9pm Tue-Thur, 6pm-9.30pm Fri & Sat, 12.30-2.30pm 5.30pm-8.30pm Sun
- **PRICE:** Dinner €56 Lunch €35
- **CREDIT CARDS:** Visa, Mastercard, Laser, Amex

- **NOTES:** Wheelchair access to restaurant. Six guestrooms. Early dinner Tue-Sat €39.

- **DIRECTIONS:**

From Cavan follow N3. At Butler's Bridge, take the N54 and the Olde Post is 3km further, on the right.
GPS 54.0801 -7.3701

CHERRY TREE RESTAURANT

Harry McKeogh
Lakeside, Ballina, Killaloe
County Clare
+353 (0) 61-375688
www.cherrytreerestaurant.ie
cherrytreerestaurant@gmail.com

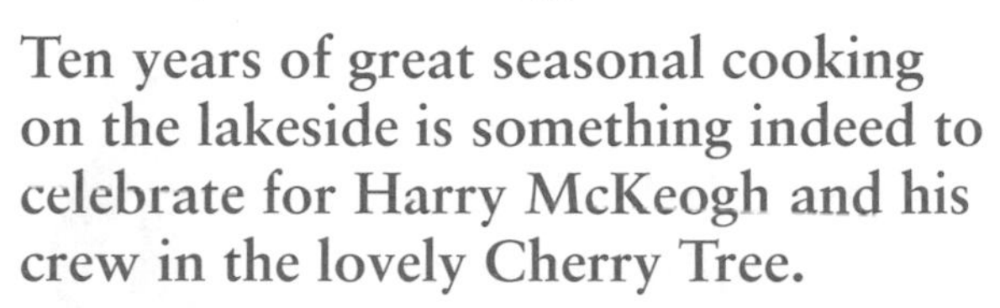

Ten years of great seasonal cooking on the lakeside is something indeed to celebrate for Harry McKeogh and his crew in the lovely Cherry Tree.

Harry McKeogh forged the template for his restaurant even before he opened his doors back in 2000, and for over a decade he has stuck with the things he knows to be good and right, the dishes that work. He returned to Clare having worked with the great Johnnie Cooke in Dublin and, like his former boss, he loves clear, clean, balanced, sweet flavours and the sort of combinations that give a dish poise, that give a dish nous, integrity. He's a smart cook, and it shows – if he makes confit of duck he puts it with ginger and sesame, because that's what works. If he fries up prawns then he congratulates their sweetness with garlic, lemon and herbs, because that's what you do. With rack of lamb, it's mint salsa verde. With beef, it's mushrooms and spinach with fondant potato. In a way, the Cherry Tree cooking is K.I.S.S. cooking – except it's not 'keep it simple, stupid'. Instead, it's keep it simple, sublime. For at its best, this food has an elegance and drama that goes beyond the ingredients, and the captivation of the food is matched by the smart, bright modern room.

- **OPEN:** 6pm-10pm Tue-Sat, 12.30pm-3pm Sun (closed Wed and Sun off season)
- **PRICE:** Set dinner from €39
- **CREDIT CARDS:** Visa, Mastercard, Laser, Amex

● NOTES:

Wheelchair access. Children's menu.

● DIRECTIONS:

Drive through Ballina village, turn left towards the bridge and right at Molly's pub, towards Lakeside Hotel.

GREGAN'S CASTLE

Simon & Freddy Haden
Ballyvaughan
County Clare
+353 (0) 65-707 7005
stay@gregans.ie
www.gregans.ie

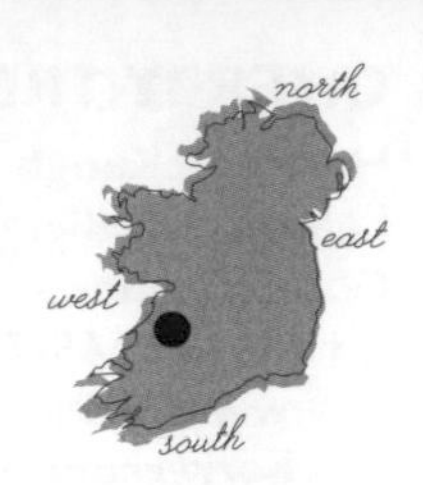

Gregan's Castle is the hottest destination in Ireland right now, and Mickael Viljanen's food is simply awesome.

"The best meal I have eaten in Ireland", says your ultra-foodie friend. "I'm going to go work a stage with this guy", says the acclaimed chef. "Never had a meal like it. He's as talented as I've ever seen", says another stellar chef. It's just as well that Mickael Viljanen is a modest, well-rooted man – he's exceptionally modest, in fact – because if he wasn't then the tsunami of praise that his cooking has won over the last two years would have fair turned his head. Gregan's is part of the pantheon of inspired Irish restaurants that have enjoyed periods of utter transcendence – Arbutus; Ballymaloe; Roscoff; Shiro; Truffles; Shanks, L'Ecrivain; Chapter One; MacNean are some others that come to mind – and the experience of staying here and eating here is simply unforgettable. Viljanen's culinary forays with superb local ingredients – egg; potato; beetroot; cod; apples – reveal a tumultuous talent, and a chef who has a philosopher's curiosity to match his artisan's graft. This is extraordinary cooking: it takes your breath away.

- **OPEN:** 6pm-9pm Mon-Sat. Seasonal Sunday menu served in Corkscrew Bar, 1pm-7pm. Bar lunch Mon-Sat 12.30pm-2pm
- **PRICE:** Dinner €65, Sun lunch €25-€35, Bar lunch from €15
- **CREDIT CARDS:** Visa, Mastercard, Laser,
- **NOTES:** Disabled access. Burren tours arranged.
- **DIRECTIONS:**

3.5miles outside Ballyvaughan village.
GPS 53.076944 -9.186222

ROADFORD HOUSE

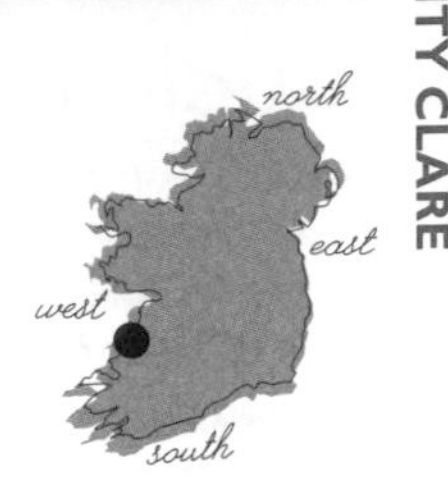

Frank & Marian Sheedy
Doolin village
County Clare
+353 (0) 65-707 5050
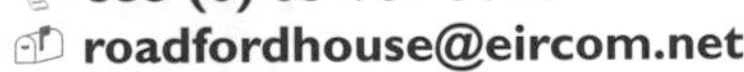
roadfordhouse@eircom.net
www.roadfordrestaurant.com

A classic him'n'her destination for eating and staying, Frank and Marian's Roadford House is just a modest, affordable, lovable delight.

It hasn't taken long for Frank Sheedy's cooking to win both critical and popular attention. At a time when culinary standards in County Clare are sky-high, here is a chef who is right up there with his peers, a cook with a lovely, sure touch, a man who signs every dish with a clear, unequivocal signature. He likes the natural sweetness of things – roast beetroot with hot smoked salmon, for example, or a pear purée with belly of pork, or sweet caramelized onion with rib-eye steak – and that touch of honey in his repertoire may explain why this food is just so enjoyable, so easy to like, so easy to enjoy. Of course, what are even easier to enjoy are the grandstanding desserts that have helped to make Roadford so appreciated, and classics such as his lemon sundae, or the lush date and rum pudding, or the brilliant summer berry trifle with chocolate crisp, show a true master at work, exhilarating patisserie that just blows your mind with brilliance. Value for money in Roadford, for both the food and their comfortable rooms, is pretty amazing. Another Clare champion.

● **OPEN:** 6pm-8.30pm/9pm each evening, closed Mon & Thur during Sep & Oct. Check off season. Closed Nov-Mar. Open Christmas.
● **PRICE:** Dinner €42
● **CREDIT CARDS:** Visa, Mastercard, Laser,

● **NOTES:** B&B available, special two-night offers available. Self-catering. Value menu, 2 courses €24.95

● **DIRECTIONS:**
In the centre of Doolin, take the slip road beside McDermott's pub. GPS 53.0202333 -9.37236666

VAUGHAN'S ANCHOR INN

Denis Vaughan
Main Street, Liscannor
County Clare
+353 (0) 65-7081548
www.vaughans.ie

info@vaughans.ie

A charming bar, an ambitious restaurant, and cosy accommodation upstairs: Denis Vaughan's Anchor Inn pretty much has all you could need.

"Ambition and competence" was how Eamon Barrett summarised the modus operandi in Denis Vaughan's pub and restaurant with rooms. Right on the money, Mr Barrett! Mr Vaughan is a hugely ambitious chef, though the ambition isn't to be rich or famous. Instead, dedicated cook that he is, the ambition is to be his best, and to do his best, with every plate he sends out from the kitchen. The ambition is, happily, matched by competence, and this kitchen rarely puts a foot wrong, even though the food reads fussy and does incline towards cheffy complexity. But, just try that roasted saddle of rabbit with foie gras and chicken mousse, rabbit pie, and lollipop with black pudding and wild mushrooms and a little rabbit jus to finish the whole shebang and it won't be the complexity or the competence that will wow! you: it will be the rich, satisfying flavours, and the pleasure of a dish built from many elements that all aim to harmonise. A pint in the bar, a smashing dinner, a comfy simple room upstairs: goodness me but that is the good life in Vaughan's Anchor Inn in County Clare.

● **OPEN:** 12.30pm-9pm Mon-Sun. Bar food daily, dinner from 6pm in restaurant.
● **PRICE:** Dinner €35, Bar Lunch mains €12-€15
● **CREDIT CARDS:** Visa, Mastercard, Laser

● **NOTES**
Wheelchair access. Accommodation available €35 per night B&B

● **DIRECTIONS:**
In the centre of Liscannor.

10 GREAT

HAPPENING ROOMS

1
THE BAY TREE
NORTHERN IRELAND

2
CLIFF HOUSE HOTEL
COUNTY WATERFORD

3
THE EXCHEQUER
COUNTY DUBLIN

4
FISHY FISHY CAFÉ
COUNTY CORK

5
HARRY'S BAR & RESTAURANT
COUNTY DONEGAL

6
JUNO'S
COUNTY DUBLIN

7
OUT OF THE BLUE
COUNTY KERRY

8
THE POACHER'S INN
COUNTY CORK

9
SAGE
COUNTY MAYO

10
VIEWMOUNT HOUSE
COUNTY LONGFORD

AUGUSTINE'S

Brendan Cashman
Lapp's Quay, City Quarter
Cork, County Cork
+353 (0) 21-427 9375
www.augustines.ie
augustinesrestaurant@gmail.com

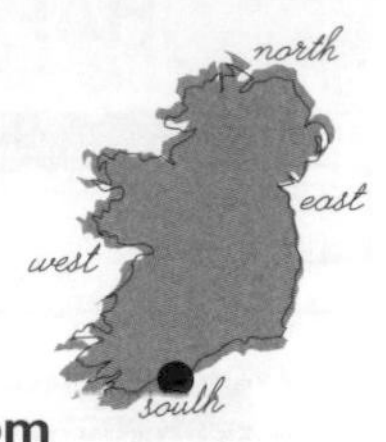

Now happily installed in the Clarion Hotel on Lapp's Quay, Brendan Cashman's restaurant is humming.

Last time Brendan Cashman featured in the *Bridgestone Guides*, he was cooking lovely food in little Toormore, in West Cork. Now, in the sleek confines of Cork's Clarion Hotel, he is back with the good stuff, writes Caroline Hennessy: "Augustine's was a bright spot of understated luxury, the room heady with the atmosphere of people enjoying a real midweek treat. Our meal kicked off in style with an unexpected amuse-bouche, a shot glass of spicy gazpacho, pure essence of tomato, set the bar high for what was to follow. There is a sure hand at work here in the kitchen: both pieces of fish that we had – sea trout to start, hake for the main – were seared to perfection with crispy skin and tender flesh. Loin of aged Irish Angus beef, a truly royal cut of meat, was similarly well treated and came complete with a dinky little steak and kidney pie that ran the risk of overshadowing the whole meal. Brendan Cashman sources ingredients from local artisan producers and the English Market, cooks them confidently and balances the flavours to perfection. Wonderful."

- **OPEN:** from 6pm Tue-Sat
- **PRICE:** Dinner €40
- **CREDIT CARDS:** Visa, Mastercard, Laser, Amex

● NOTES:
Wheelchair access with assistance.

● DIRECTIONS:
Part of the Clarion Hotel, overlooking the River Lee in the centre of Cork.

BALLYMALOE HOUSE

The Allen family
Shanagarry, Midleton
East Cork
+353 (0) 21-465 2531
www.ballymaloe.ie
res@ballymaloe.ie

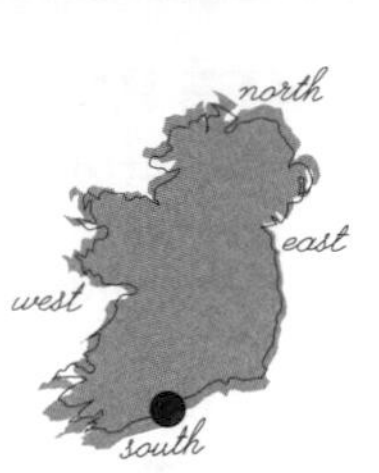

As Ballymaloe House heads towards its half-century, the grand dame of Irish food just gets better and better.

It is expensive to eat in Ballymaloe House – dinner will cost you almost 70 euros – and it may well be the best bargain in Ireland. We hate to do the old line about "What price art?', but, well, what price art? For art, and artfulness, is what you get at Ballymaloe, so don't think of dinner in this glorious old house as some transitory thing, as just another meal. Consider, instead, the murmuration of dedicated suppliers and growers and producers who farm, fish and forage all so that chef Jason Fahey can coalesce their work into magic on the plate. The magic seems simple – Ballymaloe crab paté with pickled cucumbers; guinea fowl with fresh herb stuffing; haunch of venison with Francatelli sauce and garden turnips – but it's as simple as a Morandi still-life, a William Scott pot, or a Giacometti figure. Morandi, Scott and Giacometti! Aren't we getting above ourselves here?! Not a bit of it. Art is transformation, and Ballymaloe transforms simple ingredients into works of art. The fact that it does so in one of the most delightful places to eat and stay is just another happy bonus.

● **OPEN:** 7pm-9pm dinner, 1pm-1.30pm Mon-Sun
● **PRICE:** Lunch €40, Dinner €70
● **CREDIT CARDS:** Visa, Mastercard, Laser, Amex

● **NOTES:** Wheelchair access with assistance. 33 guest rooms. Early children's dinner.

● **DIRECTIONS:**
29km east of Cork city. Take the N25 and exit for Whitegate R630, follow signs for R629 Cloyne. The House is 3km beyond Cloyne, signposted.
GPS 51.868297 -8.0837

CAFÉ PARADISO

Denis Cotter
16 Lancaster Quay
Cork, County Cork
+353 (0) 21-427 7939
www.cafeparadiso.ie
info@cafeparadiso.ie

The philosopher-king of vegetarian cookery, Denis Cotter's Café Paradiso is unique in each and every aspect.

Denis Cotter is one of those rare cooks whose musings on his profession are as accomplished as his work in the kitchen at Café Paradiso. His books and his blogs are full of pearls of hard-won, slowly-wrought philosophy. Cotter thinks slowly, and deeply, which explains why his cooking is unique – he is always trying to transcend the obvious, the clichéd. You can't make a dish such as almond pastry galette of feta and spinach with coriander crushed potato, harissa and sugar snaps without taking the repertoire of cooking apart and then making it anew, all the while getting it to sing with your own voice. So, whilst we think of cooks such as Ferran Adria and Heston Blumenthal as deconstructionists, the real deconstructionist cook is actually Denis Cotter, and he has been taking the repertoire apart in Café Paradiso since 1993. And it's not just the food that is made anew here: everything hums to Cotter's oblique, stubborn view of his art and his craft, making for the most extraordinary food in one of the most singular restaurants on little planet earth.

- **OPEN:** 5pm-10pm Tue-Sat, noon-3pm Fri & Sat
- **PRICE:** Lunch €25, Dinner €47
- **CREDIT CARDS:** Visa, Mastercard, Laser

● NOTES:

Wheelchair access, but no disabled toilet. Three guestrooms available. Pre-theatre menu Tue-Fri last orders 7pm, €24-€30

● DIRECTIONS:

Opposite the Lancaster Lodge, on your right as you head away from the city.

AN CRUIBIN & THE SILK PURSE

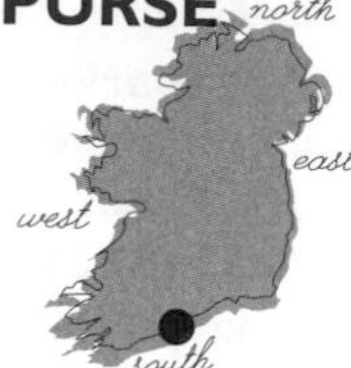

Paul Lewis & Frank O'Connell
One Union Quay
Cork, County Cork
+353 (0) 21-431 0071
www.themeatcentre.com
frank@themeatcentre.com

Paul and Frank have one motivation in life: they want to make you happy and dinner in the Silk Purse will most certainly make you happy.

They make loads of mistakes in the Silk Purse – the chilli, garlic and olive oil sauce on the fried squid slides onto the table as the waitress puts it down, and she's forgotten the bread, and the venison and lamb meat-balls could have done with a bit more seasoning – and you forgive them every mistake because there is magic here, so never mind the misses. So, the only regret about your squid sauce is that you lose some of it, because both it and the squid are so yumola, whilst hanger steak with onion and red wine is almost a masterclass in how to source and cook meat. To be honest, we actually cherish the lack of slickness in this simply unique restaurant, because any slickness would just get in the way of how heartfelt everything is, it would skew their sincerity, it would get in the way of how determined they are to cook food that will make you happy. And you will be happy with that delicious swordfish with leeks and peppers, or the smart vegetarian dishes like their orza puttanesca or the fried halloumi with baba ghanoush. A passionate silk purse.

● **OPEN:** An Cruibin open noon-midnight, Silk Purse open 6pm-10pm Thur-Sat (Wed on demand)
● **PRICE:** Meals €30, Tapas €5-€10
● **CREDIT CARDS:** Visa, Mastercard, Laser,

● **NOTES:**
Disabled access downstairs.

● **DIRECTIONS:**
Opposite the Cork City Hall, watch out for the flying pig over the door.

DEASY'S HARBOUR BAR

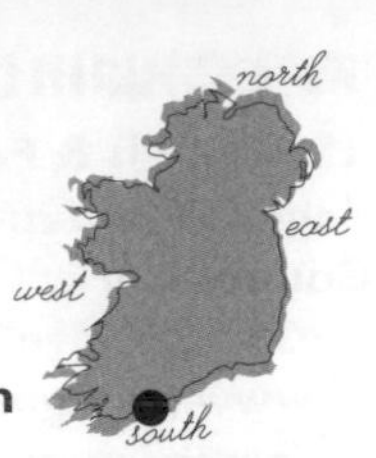

Bobby Blackwell
Ring, Clonakilty
West Cork
+353 (0) 23-883 5741
deasysrestaurant@hotmail.com
www.deasysrestaurant.ie

Caitlin Ruth's fish cookery is the star turn at the quirky, echt Deasy's, funky food you never tire of.

Something new

Caitlin Ruth's fish cookery is the lure for Clonakilty food lovers in Deasy's, an old-style pub and restaurant just across from the sea at a bend in the road, not far east of Clonakilty. In fact, it's not uncommon for them to refer to Ms Ruth as "the genius in the kitchen", but despite having a resident genius rattling the pans, Deasy's remains a laid-back place, unpretentious, casual, but blessed with sharp, stylish fish cookery. There are classics such as grilled scallops or monkfish wrapped in prosciutto, but it's often the funky excursions into global cooking, like the chard Puttanesca with hake, or the cashew and caramelised turnip cakes that show the real spirited va-va-voom of the kitchen. When we tell you that it's the sort of place and the sort of finger lickin' cooking that wins the applause of a culinary genius like our friend Clodagh McKenna, then you will see where Deasy's is coming from: good cooking, good craic, no nonsense. It gets extra busy at weekends, so make sure to have a booking if you are travelling any distance down to beautiful Clonakilty.

- **OPEN:** 6pm-9.30pm Wed-Sat, 1pm-3pm Sun
- **PRICE:** Lunch €32 Dinner €35
- **CREDIT CARDS:** Visa, Mastercard, Laser

- **NOTES:**

Limited wheelchair access. Early bird menu served 6pm-7pm, €26-€32 including a glass of wine

- **DIRECTIONS:**

Take the first left off the roundabout as you enter Clonakilty (opposite Supervalu supermarket) and follow the coastal road to Ring.

THE FARMGATE CAFÉ

Kay Harte
English Market, Cork
County Cork
+353 (0) 21-427 8134
www.farmgate.ie
farmgatecafe@yahoo.ie

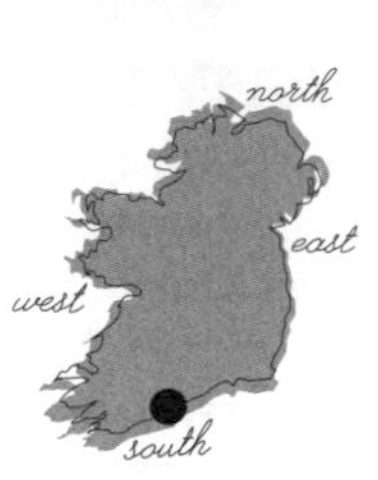

The Farm Gate's contemporary take on culinary classics from Ireland's history produces inimitable food.

Kay Harte is one of the mighty Cork Food Mavens – Cork's culinary culture is a female one, unlike the rest of the country where the culture is dominated by men – and there is no one more steadfast in asserting the value, nobility and splendour of specialist local foods than this formidable, enigmatic lady. Her daily menus present seemingly simple things: potato, thyme and wild garlic soup (the wild garlic picked by Ms Harte herself); Clare Island organic salmon; St Tola goat's cheese salad; whiting with champ; tripe and drisheen; English Market corned beef; portobello mushroom and Mossfield cheese tart; apple tart; Milleens cheese; Farmgate bread and butter pudding. Could there be anything nicer than this for lunch? Truly, we don't think so. The food in The Farmgate isn't just sustenance, it is food that also offers a philosophy, a narrative, a history, a personality, and it is offered without pretension, modestly and generously served by wonderfully characterful staff whose relish for their work is infectious. This is the real Cork cuisine, boy.

- **OPEN:** 9am-5pm Mon-Sat
- **PRICE:** Lunch €10-€16
- **CREDIT CARDS:** Visa, Mastercard, Laser

NOTES:
No wheelchair access.

DIRECTIONS:
Upstairs in the centre of Cork's English Market, which runs between Patrick Street and Oliver Plunkett Street in the city centre.

FISHY FISHY CAFE

Martin & Marie Shanahan
Crowley Quay,
Kinsale, West Cork
+353 (0) 21-470 0415
www.fishyfishy.ie
info@fishyfishy.ie

The television series, *Martin's Mad About Fish*, has made Martin Shanahan a star. In truth, he's always been a star.

Of course, as we have written about him for years, we can always say: "Sure, we knew Martin Shanahan before he was famous". That's what they would say in Cork, whilst Dubliners would simply say: "Martin Shanahan? Sure I know him!".

Mr Shanahan has been famous amongst food lovers for some time, but his marvellous television series, "Martin's Mad About Fish" has seen the beginning of the ascent of this charming man to what will be national fame. He deserves it. Mr Shanahan is straight-talking, yet he is also reverential about fish, cooking fish, serving fish, enjoying fish. He is, indeed, mad about fish, and if you eat at Fishy Fishy, where business has shown another stratospheric increase in the past year, you will understand that it is this passion for his beloved raw ingredients from the sea that makes this fish cookery so special, so complete, so elemental. There is no better experience in Irish food than to be sat in Fishy Fishy on a warm afternoon, or a sunny early-evening, eating the blessings of the ocean. Start with the crab cocktail!

● **OPEN:** noon-9pm Mon-Sun Mar-Oct, noon-4pm Mon-Thu, noon-9pm Fri & Sat, noon-5pm Sun Oct-Mar. Always phone to check off season.
● **PRICE:** Meals €35
● **CREDIT CARDS:** Visa, Mastercard

● **NOTES:**
Wheelchair access. Fishy Fishy Shop and Chippie now open +353 (0) 21-477 4453.

● **DIRECTIONS:**
On the waterfront near Acton's Hotel.

GOOD THINGS CAFÉ

Carmel Somers
Ahakista Road, Durrus
West Cork
+353 (0) 27-61426
www.thegoodthingscafe.com
info@thegoodthingscafe.com

Carmel Somers draws from culinary history as well as the culinary hinterland to fashion thrilling food in Good Things.

Carmel Somers learnt her craft from two little-known but much respected English cooks, Colin White, and Stephen Markwick. Like her mentors, whom she has described as "Good, honest, kind cooks", she herself is a cult figure, and she also cooks a cuisine which is, in many ways, not of its time – omelette Arnold Bennett; lobster with garlic, parsley and lemon; lamb kidneys with lime butter; poached cherries with vanilla ice cream. The food in Good Things may not be fashionable, but it is, indeed, good, honest, and kind. It is cooking that is led by ingredients, by interpretation, but also led by history, led by that great school of cookery enshrined by Elizabeth David, Jane Grigson, Patience Grey, and by White and Markwick. Ms Somers carries the mantle of this good and honest cooking, in this little room at the edge of Dunmanus Bay, and it is one of those places where magic can happen, where the day and the food and the wine coalesce into something that is sensual, sensuous, and maybe even spiritual. Unique, and Pure West Cork, of course.

- **OPEN:** 11.30am-4pm, 6.30pm-9pm Thur-Mon. Open Easter, bank hol weekends, and from 21 Jun-1 Sep. Open Fri nights off season.
- **PRICE:** Lunch €19, Dinner €45
- **CREDIT CARDS:** Visa, Mastercard, Laser

NOTES:
Wheelchair access. Shop selling produce and cookery books. Cookery classes.

DIRECTIONS:
On the Ahakista road just outside the village.

10 PLACES

WITH GREAT SERVICE

1. THE CHINA SICHUAN
   COUNTY DUBLIN

2. THE FARM GATE CAFÉ
   COUNTY CORK

3. GRANGECON CAFÉ
   COUNTY WICKLOW

4. HARRY'S BAR AND RESTAURANT
   COUNTY DONEGAL

5. KELLY'S RESORT HOTEL
   COUNTY WEXFORD

6. MACNEAN RESTAURANT
   COUNTY CAVAN

7. MICHIE SUSHI
   COUNTY DUBLIN

8. O'BRIEN CHOP HOUSE
   COUNTY WATERFORD

9. THE OLDE POST INN
   COUNTY CAVAN

10. PACKIES
    COUNTY KERRY

LONGUEVILLE HOUSE

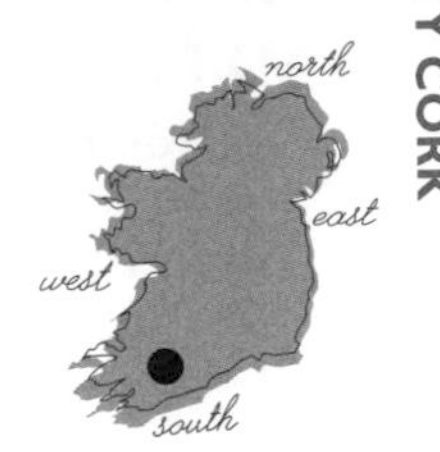

William & Aisling O'Callaghan
The President's Restaurant
Mallow, North Cork
+353 (0) 22-47156
www.longuevillehouse.ie
info@longuevillehouse.ie

Caroline Hennessy enjoyed the theatre that is dinner in north Cork's celebrated Longueville House.

Dining at Longueville House – and it is dining, not a mere dinner – is an experience. Your evening starts when you turn into the long, winding drive. After passing through mature woods, you emerge at the front of the house, perfectly positioned to take in its magnificent setting in the Blackwater Valley. The scene, even before you have crunched across the gravel and passed through the enormous, heavy door, is well set. Menus, drinks and nibbles in the beautiful drawing room is an opportunity to relax and appreciate the surroundings before being shown to a table in the elegant President's Restaurant. Chef William O'Callaghan has an intimate relationship with his ingredients, many of which are drawn from the estate. Vegetables, fruit and herbs come from the walled garden, the beef and lamb on your plate is reared in situ, Longueville apple brandy features on the menu and fish – mackerel and salmon – come home-smoked. It's very definitely a night out, a chance to play lord of the manor.

- **OPEN:** Dinner Wed-Sun Apr-Dec, Fri-Sat Jan-Mar
- **PRICE:** Dinner €40-€90
- **CREDIT CARDS:** Visa, Mastercard, Laser, Amex

- **NOTES:** Limited wheelchair access. Recommended for vegetarians. Hotel will open off season for groups of 20 or more

- **DIRECTIONS:**

5km from Mallow when travelling in direction of Killarney, and well signposted from the road.
GPS 52.133515 -8.720934

MAD FISH

Denis Cronin
1 Point Road, Crosshaven
County Cork
+353 (0) 21-483 1829
info@croninspub.com
www.croninspub.com

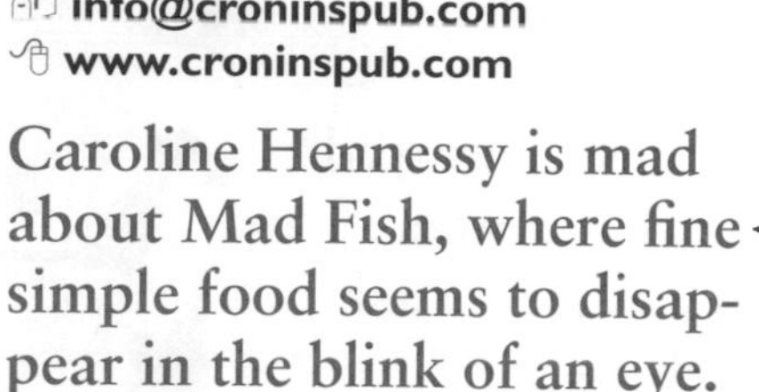

Caroline Hennessy is mad about Mad Fish, where fine simple food seems to disappear in the blink of an eye.

"Tucked into a cosy backroom at Cronin's Pub, this is the kind of establishment that makes you feel all warm inside", says Caroline Hennessy. "Unpretentious and relaxed, there's no fuss about the food but the proof of quality is in the speed of its disappearance. Crispy rings of salt and pepper squid, dipped in a chilli-lime aioli, hardly spent a moment on the table before they were gone. Chilli cream shrimp got the same treatment, as well as a call for a spoon to slurp up the last of the juices. A simple fillet of baked hake came with perfectly blackened butter for anointing and a large dish of curly kale and mashed potatoes to fill any gaps. Meat eaters are also well catered for: the sister happily tucked into a sirloin steak, sourced from Durcan's Meats in the English Market, compete with all the trimmings, and then some. This is the kind of place that any 'just give me a good feed' Dad would like – large portions, plenty of spuds and good prices – while his food-loving daughters are kept more than happy with careful food sourcing and some damn fine cooking."

- **OPEN:** 6pm-9pm Thu-Sat
- **PRICE:** Dinner €30
- **CREDIT CARDS:** Visa, Mastercard, Laser, Amex

● NOTES:
Limited wheelchair access. Cronin's serves food noon-2.45pm Mon-Fri, noon-3.30pm Sat, 1pm-4.30pm Sun

● DIRECTIONS:
Part of Cronin's pub which is in the centre of Crosshaven. Crosshaven is just south of Cork city at the entrance to Cork Harbour.

O'CALLAGHAN-WALSHE

Sean Kearney
The Square, Rosscarbery
West Cork
+353 (0) 23-8848125
fun.fish@hotmail.com

The West Cork seafood treasures found on the doorstep of O'C-W are magnificently transformed in this ace place.

Some people don't get the insouciant brilliance of O'C-W. We guess that if you want conventional restaurants rather than singular restaurants, and if you expect clichéd service rather than sublime service, then you won't get the point of this iconic West Cork destination. If you think a restaurant should be the way you want, and should do things the way you want, rather than being the way it is, and doing things the way it does, then O'Callaghan-Walshe won't be your dream date. But if you admire a certain lugubriousness of style and a certain cussedness of manner, and if you love great fish and shellfish cookery, then O'C-W will seem to you to be the fish restaurant from heaven. Sean and Martina do what they do, and nobody does what they do the way they do it. We applaud this originality, and we crave this superb cooking: the perfect mashed potatoes; the clean, smooth watercress sauce with john dory; the best scampi in West Cork; the selection of simple, perfectly executed puddings. And, if you follow Sean's advice with the wines, satisfaction is assured.

- **OPEN:** 6.30pm-9.30pm Tue-Sun. Weekends only Oct-May
- **PRICE:** Dinner €35-€40
- **CREDIT CARDS:** Visa, Mastercard, Laser

● NOTES:
Wheelchair access, but no disabled toilet. Reservations recommended. Vegetarians please pre-book.

● DIRECTIONS:
On the main square in Rosscarbery. In the centre of the village, turn off at the Celtic Ross hotel.

THE POACHER'S INN

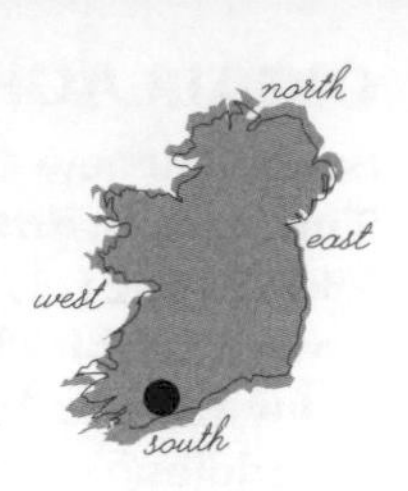

Barry & Catherine McLoughlin
Clonakilty Road, Bandon
County Cork
+353 (0) 23-884 1159
www.poachersinnbandon.com
info@poachersinnbandon.com

Barry and Catherine's fish restaurant offers brilliant fish cookery, and service that makes you smile.

Step inside the Poacher's, and just look at how everything sparkles, from the gleaming white plates to the bottles of their own mineral water. It's a sure sign of the care lavished on each detail of running this hugely popular restaurant and gastropub on the Clonakilty road just on the edge of Bandon. Barry McLoughlin spent time working in the kitchens of Fishy Fishy Café in Kinsale with Martin Shanahan, and he knows how to present a plate at its optimum, whether it's their classic West Cork seafood tapas – perfect squid in chilli sauce; fresh prawns with avocado; beautiful gratin of crab; a shot of rich chowder and fine brown soda bread – the seafood pie with cod, mussels, clams and prawns; roasted hake with Barryroe potatoes; or striploin steak with mash and mushrooms. Catherine looks after everyone as if she has known them all her life, and the net result is a seafood bar and restaurant that really cares about everything they do, and that really cares that you should have the best possible time. The McLoughlins show exactly how to run a great house.

● **OPEN:** Restaurant open 7pm-11pm Thur-Sat. Barfood open noon-3pm, 5.30pm-9pm Mon-Thu, noon-9pm Fri & Sat, 12.30pm-7.30pm Sun
● **PRICE:** Bar Menu €15, Restaurant Dinner €30
● **CREDIT CARDS:** Visa, Mastercard, Laser, Amex

● **NOTES:**
Limited wheelchair access to bar. Menu of cooked party food to eat at home.

● **DIRECTIONS:**
Just outside the town on the Clonakilty Road.

TODDIE'S @THE BULMAN

Pearse & Mary O'Sullivan
Summercove, Kinsale, West Cork
+353 (0) 21-477 2131/477 7769
www.toddies.ie
www.thebullman.com
toddies@eircom.net

The move to the Bulman has been the best thing that has ever happened to Toddie's, and Pearse & Mary are on top form in this ace waterside place.

The Bulman Bar at Summercove has been the third different Kinsale location for Toddie's restaurant, and it has proven to be the best. This classic bar and restaurant has allowed Pearse O'Sullivan to show the twin characteristics of his cooking: simpler food in the bar, and slightly more formal, slightly more polished cooking upstairs in the restaurant. The bar food is 'just-what-I-wanted' grub: coronation chicken tortilla; Ummera smoked chicken salad; Bulman burger and chips, food that perfectly gives you exactly what you want in a great room, and you can tell just how much Mr O'Sullivan loves getting this punchy, tasty food just right. Upstairs offers a smashing room, and more smashing food: spring rolls of Bluebell Falls goat's cheese; carpaccio of Hereford beef with Desmond cheese; Dromoland estate wood pigeon with a bean cassoulet; fillet steak with pumpkin purée; scallops with pea and mint risotto. Joyful cooking in a joyful, energised enterprise with a joyful, energised atmosphere. Don't miss this hotshot, a blast of pure Kinsale energy.

● **OPEN:** 6.30pm-10.30pm Mon-Sat, Bar lunch Mon-Sun 12.30pm-5pm. Check off season.
● **PRICE:** Dinner €40 Lunch from €10
● **CREDIT CARDS:** Visa, Mastercard, Laser, Amex

● **NOTES:**
Wheelchair access.

● **DIRECTIONS:**
Five minute drive, fifteen minute walk, from Kinsale town, at foot of hill before Charles Fort.

AN BONNAN BUI

Martin & Monica Kelly
Pier Road, Rathmullan
County Donegal
+353 (0) 74-915 8453
www.anbonnanbui.com
bonnanbui@yahoo.ie

Just about as far north as you can travel in Ireland, An Bonnan Bui is worth the journey to sample Monica's food, and that famous chocolate cake.

Simple things can make you famous. Martin Kelly and Monica Santos's lovely, simple An Bonnan Bui in little Rathmullan is famous for: the chocolate cake. They could describe the cake as "the world-famous chocolate cake". But that's not their style. Instead it's described as "a very good chocolate cake". But it is much more than that, as indeed is everything this talented pair cook and serve. Monica's Brazilian background shows itself in the menus, but whether she is preparing her native dishes or more conventional fare, such as rack of lamb or Mulroy Bay scallops, the cooking is precise, expert, superbly defined. You can enjoy everything here from Middle Eastern kibbeh to Brazilian seafood specials, and it is all cooked with sure understanding and modesty, though the seafood specials are pretty hard to resist: crab, leek and chilli cakes; spicy whitebait; local plaice with a basil and cherry tomato vinaigrette; monkfish with a chilli, garlic and coriander butter. And, of course, it is all a prelude to that world-famous chocolate cake, a prelude to a chocolate kiss.

- **OPEN:** Mon-Sun 6pm-9.30pm, 1pm-5pm Sun. Open weekends only off season.
- **PRICE:** Dinner €30-€40
- **CREDIT CARDS:** Visa, Mastercard, Laser

● NOTES:
Full wheelchair access once you've negotiated the steps into the restaurant. Early Bird menu, 6pm-7pm, €23

● DIRECTIONS:
Head down main street to the shore, but instead of driving down to the beach turn left onto Pier Road.

AROMA

Tom Dooley & Arturo de Alba
Donegal Craft Village
Donegal, County Donegal
+353 (0) 74-972 3222
tomandarturo@yahoo.com
www.donegalcraftvillage.com/aroma.html

With a new Aroma in the centre of Donegal town proving a smash hit, Tom and Arturo's Aroma is showing a new raft of customers their brilliance.

Back in the day, we used to receive little hand-written notes here at Bridgestone Central, written and posted by food lovers to alert us to something interesting, often not even signed. And so it was several years back that we received a little slip of paper telling us that we should check out Aroma. And we went along, and we ate the best dish we ate in all of 2005 – if you have a memory for this sort of thing, you will recall that it was a risotto with white wine, asparagus and Parmesan. We sat in this little room and marvelled at how such precise cooking could happen in such a little place, and we bought some brown bread and when we got home and tasted it we wondered how on earth such marvellous baking could take place in such a little space. Since then Tom – the baker – and Arturo – the chef – haven't looked back. They have gone from strength to strength. They have opened a second branch in Donegal town itself. Their breads and baking are the stuff of legend, they attract a celebrity audience to this little room, and they do everything with TLC.

● **OPEN:** 9am-5.30pm, lunch served noon-4pm Mon-Sat. Aroma 2 closes at 5pm. Aroma 1 closed Jan & Feb.
● **PRICE:** Lunch €18.50
● **CREDIT CARDS:** Visa, Mastercard, Laser

● **NOTES:** Wheelchair access both. Aroma 2, Mill Row, Donegal town Tel 074-972 3456

● **DIRECTIONS:**
Craft Village is clearly signposted, 2km or so south of the town centre. Aroma 2 is in the town centre, in front of the famous Magee factory.

10 PLACES

TO BEAT THE RECESSION

1
AUGUSTINE'S
COUNTY CORK

2
THE BROWN BEAR
COUNTY KILDARE

3
BROWN'S
COUNTY LONDONDERRY

4
THE COTTAGE RESTAURANT
COUNTY LEITRIM

5
HARRY'S BAR & RESTAURANT
COUNTY DONEGAL

6
THE HOUSE
COUNTY DUBLIN

7
JUNO'S
COUNTY DUBLIN

8
THE MILL RESTAURANT
COUNTY DONEGAL

9
THORNTON'S
COUNTY DUBLIN

10
TODDIES AT THE BULMAN
COUNTY CORK

HARRY'S BAR & RESTAURANT

Donal & Kevin Doherty
Bridgend, Inishowen
County Donegal
+353 (0) 74-936 8544

info@harrys.ie
www.harrys.ie

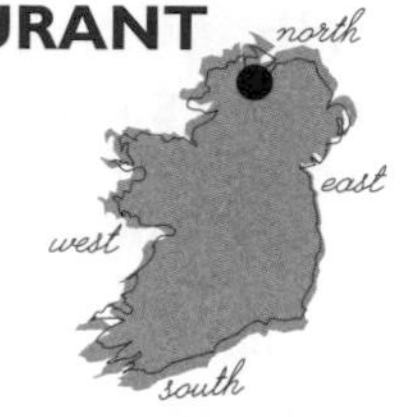

Donal Doherty is one of the most important players in Irish food and, with chef Ray Moran, Harry's is just making magic.

Every so often an Irish restaurant transcends itself, and gets into a space where the magic happens with every service. Harry's is in that place. Donal Doherty's one-man crusade to source the finest Donegal foods, and chef Raymond Moran's skill in interpreting creative dishes with those ingredients, is making for one of the mightiest food experiences in Ireland. The tribe of McKennas had dinner here twice on our Inishowen trip, and we were blown away twice by a cuisine that is so logical, so pure, so complete, that it means Harry's takes its place right up there with the hottest restaurants in Ireland. Everything was outstanding – the stuffed Greencastle squid; the crab pannacotta; the Inishowen pâtés; the breaded langoustines; the Inishowen lamb; the Greencastle fish. And, of course, their incredible beef steaks, which have no equal, so fine we were stunned into silence, until P J McKenna said; "To quote Homer Simpson, this is what angels must taste like!" Angels dancing on your tongue, that's what you get at Harry's, along with great service and incredible value.

● **OPEN:** noon-4pm, 4pm-9pm Mon-Sun, open 'till 10pm Fri & Sat. Closed 8pm Mon-Tue winter hours.
● **PRICE:** Lunch specials €9, Sunday lunch €18.95, Dinner €17-€27
● **CREDIT CARDS:** Visa, Mastercard, Laser

● **NOTES:** Wheelchair access. Early bird menu 2-courses for €16, Mon-Fri

● **DIRECTIONS:**
On the main N13 between Derry and Buncrana.
GPS 55.03995 -7.3774

THE MILL RESTAURANT

Derek & Susan Alcorn
Figart, Dunfanaghy
North Donegal
+353 (0) 74-913 6985
www.themillrestaurant.com
themillrestaurant@oceanfree.net

Derek Alcorn is a star chef, yet he remains by and large unknown, except by his loyal, devoted customers.

Derek Alcorn is one of those chefs who simply has the touch, the fluency, the balance and the maturity to turn everything he cooks into a quiet little drama.
He loves to spin things in unexpected ways, so his partners for crispy pork belly are tabbouleh and soy sauce – who else would do that, who else could see that that trio would work! He does the same with Horn Head crab, where he makes a sweetcorn sorbet to act as a foil for the avocado that comes with the dish. He thinks a lot about his cooking, and we all benefit, thanks to inspired ideas such as aubergine and sultana gravy with duck, or the cardamom sauce with Greencastle turbot. We have said before that, were he cooking in the capital, he would be famous, so fine and original is his work. But instead he works quietly away in Dunfanaghy, with a happy kitchen team – name-checked on the menu! – and with a suite of comfortable rooms above the pretty restaurant in this lovely house for guests to enjoy. That's the way you become a great chef: do your best, quietly, modestly, serenely.

● **OPEN:** 7pm-9pm Tue-Sun (closed Halloween-Easter. Weekends only Mar-Apr)
● **PRICE:** Dinner €43.50
● **CREDIT CARDS:** Visa, Mastercard, Laser, Amex

● **NOTES:** Wheelchair access to restaurant. Recommended for children. Six guestrooms.

● **DIRECTIONS:**
From Letterkenny take the N56 through Dunfanaghy. The Mill is 1km past the village on right.
GPS 55.176856 -7.980311

ANANDA RESTAURANT

Asheesh Dewan
Sandyford Road
Dundrum Town Centre, Dublin 14
+353 (0) 1-296 0099
info@anandarestaurant.ie
www.anandarestaurant.ie

Ananda has pioneered new standards of Indian cookery, with levels of style and service to match the super food.

Even hell – for which read the ghastly Dundrum Shopping Centre – can have an oasis of calm and creativity, and in the DSC that oasis is the brilliant Ananda. Asheesh Dewan has fashioned new standards of creativity and achievement for Indian cooking here, in a beautiful room that is one of the treasures of the southside. Don't come to Ananda to eat the conventional dishes that must, of necessity, appear on the menu. Instead chase the voodoo down in some of their stunning fusion dishes – chicken stuffed with morels and pistachio in a morel-infused korma; lamb with parsnip purée and roganjosh; potato cake with black gram and raw mango powder; spice crusted scallops with coconut risotto and crisp bacon. You haven't tasted anything quite like this, believe us, and the fact that the children's menu is only brilliant, and very affordable, means that the young food lovers can have a taste of the real thing. The room is lovely, and proper service brings the curtain down on one of the very hottest, most happening Dublin destinations. *CB*

- **OPEN:** 5.30pm-11pm Mon-Sun, 12.30pm-3pm Thur-Sun.
- **PRICE:** Dinner €40-€45
- **CREDIT CARDS:** Visa, Mastercard, Laser, Amex

- **NOTES:**

Wheelchair access. Children's Platter recommended. Early bird 5.30pm-7pm

- **DIRECTIONS:**

Part of the Dundrum Shopping Centre, on the second floor of the cinema complex.

BON APPETIT

Oliver Dunne
9 St James Terrace
Malahide, County Dublin
+353 (0) 1-845 0314
www.bonappetit.ie
info@bonappetit.ie

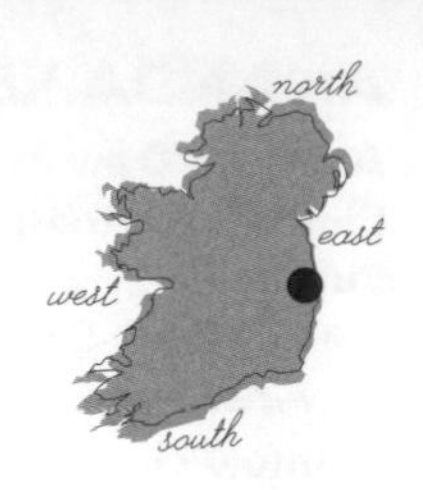

Whether you choose the bistro or the more formal restaurant, Bon Appetit's food is unified by Oliver Dunne's brilliance

Oliver Dunne is creating one of the city's glories in Bon Appetit. His food is involved, precise, challenging to both the senses and the intellect, and very, very expert in terms of delivery on the plate: warm salad of rabbit, globe artichokes, broad beans and cep vinaigrette, or pan-fried brill with roasted cauliflower and lime purée, celery gnocchi and red wine sauce, are typical of his improvisations with texture and flavour, and the food never misses a beat. Mr Dunne is one of the best cooks of his generation, and the creativity and originality of his dishes is a total thrill, with flavours, textures and colours all summoned with a painterly, pointillist perfection. His cuisine takes many elements of the modern style – taste essays in lamb, or quail, or rare-breed pork, or prawns or polenta, or chocolate – but at heart he is a straight-ahead cook, and he doesn't get lost in the maze of needless complication: he is a disciplined chef, and cooks disciplined food. Prices are very fair for such original work, with great value. *CB*

● **OPEN:** Brasserie open 6pm-10.30pm Mon-Sat, 1pm-8pm Sun; Restaurant open 7pm-9.30pm Tue-Sat, 12.30pm-2.30pm Fri
● **PRICE:** Dinner €65-€80, Brasserie Dinner €30, Lunch €22.95-€25
● **CREDIT CARDS:** Visa, Mastercard, Laser, Amex

● **NOTES:**
No wheelchair access. Early bird menu from €22.95

● **DIRECTIONS:**
In the Georgian Terrace in front of the estuary.

CHAPTER ONE

Ross Lewis & Martin Corbett
18-19 Parnell Square
Dublin 1
+353 (0) 1-873 2266
www.chapteronerestaurant.com
info@chapteronerestaurant.com

north
east
west
south
hot

Ross and Martin and all the team in Chapter One are the envy of their peers. They earn, and deserve, all that respect.

The thing about Ross Lewis is this: he's always smiling. Anytime you see a shot of him in the 'paper or in a magazine, he's smiling like a sandboy. He's a happy dude! Other chefs want to appear serious or moody, or even mean. But Mr Lewis just beams. Maybe one of the reasons why he smiles so much is because he knows that he is respected. Not just by his customers – they don't respect him: they adore him – but also by his colleagues. "Ross runs Chapter One for guests", says Garrett Byrne of Campagne, himself a guy who toiled here. "Anybody can have a restaurant serving great food but to run one having great service and atmosphere as well is the hardest thing possible in this business. Ross and the guys do it day in, day out, year in, year out" Too right, Garrett. Service, atmosphere, and food that defines the limits and the potential of modern Irish cooking. Our last meal here featured the best cooking we have ever experienced in Chapter One, and right from the day they opened in 1992, Ross, Martin and the team have kept improving, kept smiling.

- **OPEN:** 12.30pm-2pm Tue-Fri; 6pm-10pm Tue-Sat
- **PRICE:** Lunch €30-€37.50, Dinner €60
- **CREDIT CARDS:** Visa, Mastercard, Laser

- **NOTES:** Limited wheelchair access - basement restaurant.Pre-theatre, 6pm-7.40pm, €37.50

- **DIRECTIONS:**

In the basement of the Dublin Writers' Museum, on the North side of the city.
GPS 53.354269 -6.263783

CHINA SICHUAN

Kevin Hui
The Forum, Ballymoss Road
Sandyford, Dublin 18
+353 (0) 1-293 5100
www.china-sichuan.ie
info@china-sichuan.ie

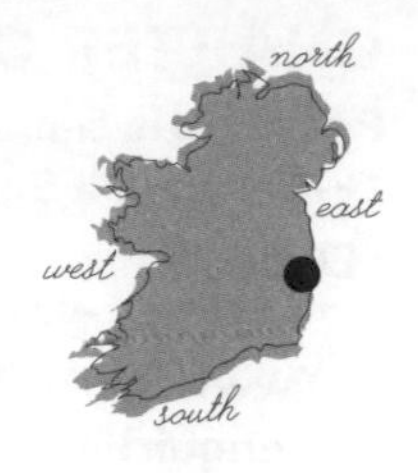

Back with a bang, Kevin Hui's restaurant takes its place at the pinnacle of accomplished ethnic cooking.

When the China Sichuan closed its doors in early 2010, the shock waves amongst food lovers were seismic. When it re-opened those doors several months later, the relief amongst food lovers was volcanic. Welcome back, baby: we missed you, we sure missed you. In fact, we had one of our most profound learning experiences in the original kitchen of the CS many, many years ago, when we watched as the chef made half a dozen dishes in as many minutes. To this day, we have still never seen comparable speed or skill in any professional kitchen, and today those skills are used to create ethnic cooking that is unlike any other in Ireland. You can order relatively conventional food here, but that would be a pity when you could enjoy their classic Sichuan dishes such as spicy Ma Po tofu, or twice-cooked belly pork with chilli, or rabbit with green tea leaves or boiled spicy beef with pak choi or camphor tea smoked duck. The room is bright and airy, the Stillorgan LUAS line is a hundred metres from the door, and it's great to have the Hui family's China Sichuan back.

- **OPEN:** noon-3pm Mon-Fri, 5pm-10pm Mon-Sat, noon-9pm Sun
- **PRICE:** Lunch €15, Dinner €30
- **CREDIT CARDS:** All major cards accepted.

● NOTES:
Wheelchair access. Value menu €20

● DIRECTIONS:
Just off the M50 and 100 yards from the Stillorgan Luas stop.

L'ECRIVAIN

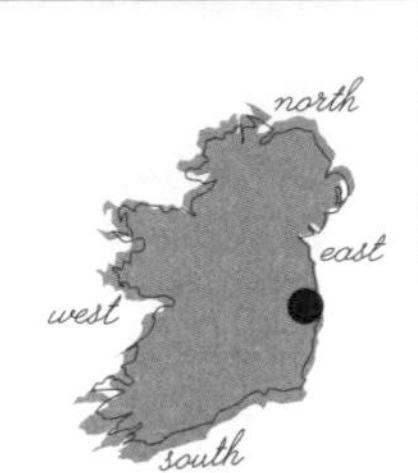

Derry & Sallyanne Clarke
109 Lower Baggot Street
Dublin 2
+353 (0) 1-661 1919
www.lecrivain.com
enquiries@lecrivain.com

A gentlemanly restaurant run by a gentleman, L'Ecrivain is supremely benign and endearing, with killer cooking.

We have written about Derry Clarke for nigh on two decades now, but we have never adverted to one of the central aspects of his character that graces both his cooking, and his celebrated restaurant. To put it simply, Mr Clarke has a bit of the aristocrat about him. He is a confident, big guy who knows who he is, and that confidence in his own skills explains why he has been such a success for two decades, and explains why he is at the pinnacle of his profession. Mind you, being somewhat aristocratic in nature won't cut much mustard unless your cooking is right up there, and the L'Ecrivain cooking is indeed right up there. Our last dinner – a small Bridgestone event in the private dining room – showcased superlative Irish foods – scallops; john dory; crubeens; Hereford beef; pannacotta – in a stunning succession of creative oompah. The evening was brilliant, and showed a restaurant of the top calibre. It also showed a restaurateur who is supremely generous, whose nobility obliges him to show his ingredients at their very best. Noblesse oblige.

● **OPEN:** 12.30pm-2pm Mon-Fri; 6.30pm-10.30pm Mon-Sat. Closed Tue and Wed lunch off season.
● **PRICE:** Lunch from €25, Dinner €65-€85
● **CREDIT CARDS:** Visa, Mastercard, Laser, Amex

● **NOTES:** Limited wheelchair access on ground floor. Private dining room.

● **DIRECTIONS:**
Through a small archway, just beside Lad Lane, across the road from Bank of Ireland HQ on Baggot Street. GPS 53.336131 -6.248619

ELY

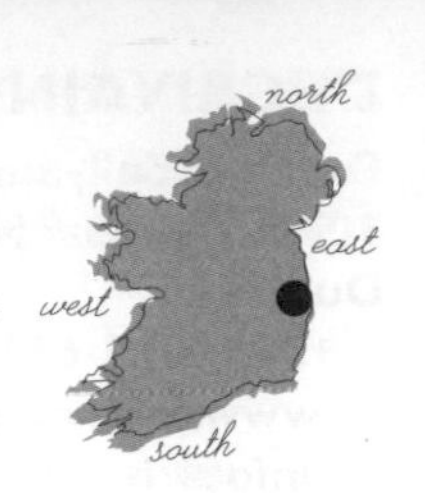

Erik Robson & Michelle Moyles
●Ely Wine Bar, 22 Ely Place, D2 +353 (0) 1-676 8986 ●Ely CHQ, IFSC, D1 & 672 0010 ●Ely HQ Gastro pub, Hanover Quay, D2 & 633 9986 www.elywinebar.ie

Three great destinations, all of them different, yet all united by a vivid, fun, uncontrived, ELY aesthetic.

Ely celebrated a decade in business at the very end of 2009, a decade during which Erik and Michelle Robson's wine bars have become some of the key destinations in the city. What's to explain the regard in which they are held? You can talk about their magnificent wines, and their lovely, beautifully realised Irish comfort food. You might mention that they are amongst the quintessential "Providers of good times", which the normally somewhat sober *Financial Times* pin-pointed as a key part of their appeal. But for us, Ely is characterised by its staff, who are up-front, up-beat, classy and friendly, as well as being awesomely on top of their game, and it is from these young folk that the energy of the trinity of Elys emerge, led from the front by the Robsons. The proof of the Ely pudding is the fact that, having got the right format in design, drinks and food, when they opened, Erik and Michelle have had to do little or no tweaking with their original concept. The only thing the punter has to do is to decide which of the three is your favourite: Ely Original? Ely CHQ? Ely HQ?

● **OPEN:** Elys open for lunch and dinner. Exact opening times for each restaurant available on web.
● **PRICE:** Lunch €10-€15, Dinner €16-€25
● **CREDIT CARDS:** Visa, Mastercard, Laser, Amex

● **NOTES:**
Wheelchair access in both CHQ and HQ.

● **DIRECTIONS:**
Ely Place is at the juncton of Baggot St and Merrion St, just off St Stephen's Green. CHQ is north of the River Liffey, beside IFSC. HQ overlooks Hanover Quay.

THE EXCHEQUER

Peter Rock & Ian Tucker
3-5 Exchequer Street
Dublin 2
+353 (0) 1-670 6787
www.theexchequer.ie
info@theexchequer.ie

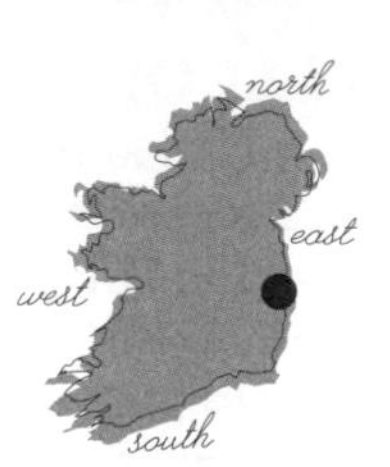

Peter and Ian's gastropub is what an Irish gastropub should be: great food, drinks, value and service.

"The Exchequer is what the Irish pub scene needed, and needs more of", says Caroline Byrne. "It's a seriously good bar, with a drinks list boasting a nice selection of decent wines by the glass, an admirable line-up of beers and spirits that goes way beyond the typical offering (especially for rum fans), and a fine lot of outstanding cocktails created by resident champion mixologist Darren Gerraghty. It also does seriously good food: hearty and great value, offering a broad range from classics – such as Doran's smoked chowder with potato and leek – to original and innovative dishes that combine great Irish ingredients to create things of pure deliciousness, like the moreish Irish whiskey and apricot bread and butter pudding with honey and ginger ice cream. The Exchequer also does a terrific deal on a Sunday roast (rib of beef for two, rack of pork or roast chicken for four) with all the trimmings and a bottle of house wine for only 40 euro. Peter and Ian know how to do gastropub, and they're doing it brilliantly. Behold the Irish gastropub, and how it should be done". CB.

● **OPEN:** 12pm-11.30pm Mon-Thurs, noon-2.30am Fri & Sat, noon-11pm Sun.
● **PRICE:** Lunch €15, Dinner €30
● **CREDIT CARDS:** Visa, Mastercard, Amex, Laser

● **NOTES:**
No wheelchair access. Breakfast served 7.30am-10am Mon-Fri, 8am-10.30am Sat & Sun

● **DIRECTIONS:**
Just off South Great George's Street in the centre of the city.

FALLON & BYRNE

Fiona McHugh & Paul Byrne
Exchequer Building
11-17 Exchequer Street, Dublin 2
+353 (0) 1-472 1010
www.fallonandbyrne.com
feedback@fallonandbyrne.com

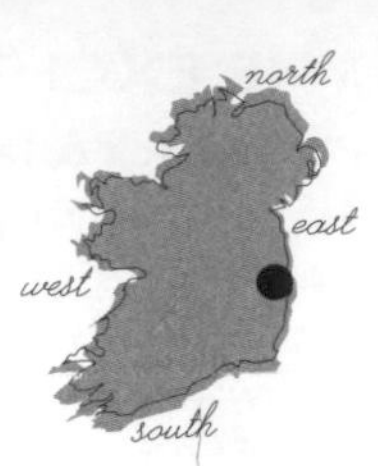

The cherry on the icing on the cake of a special morning in Dublin: a Fallon & Byrne moment to treasure forever.

A summer morning, and Connie, PJ and John McKenna are having the best sort of Dublin morning, shopping for water sport gear in the sunshine, taking coffee and hot chocolate at Fallon & Byrne, checking out the shoes in Schuh and the hiking gear in Patagonia, buying the Kelly's Hotel art book in Avoca. Lovely, quite lovely, one of those mornings when Dublin is at its best, all youthful, friendly, relaxed. So, how do you bring the perfect morning to a perfect conclusion? Lunch in Fallon & Byrne, of course. So, up the stairs we go, into that lovely light-filled room, and we have the veal bolognaise with linguini, the potato gnocchi with roasted cherry tomatoes and lemon emulsion, the leek linguini with grilled courgettes and Parmesan. Glasses of home-made lemonade; a scoop of white wine for Dad, and it takes us all back to our first ever visit to this great emporium, a Saturday night family dinner sat at the bar, with the room at its most beautifully raucous. Fallon & Byrne. Let it into your life, and you can't get it out of your life. And that's the place to have it.

● **OPEN:** noon-3pm Mon-Fri, noon-4pm Sun, 6pm-9pm Mon-Tue, till 10pm Wed-Thur, till 11pm Fri & Sat
● **PRICE:** Lunch €18.50-€23, Dinner €45
● **CREDIT CARDS:** Visa, Mastercard, Laser, Amex

● **NOTES:**
Full wheelchair access. Pre-theatre dinner menu, at 6pm or 6.30pm, €25-€30

● **DIRECTIONS:**
Exchequer St leads off Wicklow St, which itself leads off Dublin's main shopping street, Grafton St.

HOT CHEFS TO WATCH

1

FRED CORDONNIER
THE BROWN BEAR

2

DAVIDE DANNALOIA
SAGE

3

RAYMOND MORAN
HARRY'S BAR & RESTAURANT

4

JESS MURPHY
BAR NO 8

5

GARY O'HANLON
VIEWMOUNT HOUSE

6

MICHEL PIARE
MICHIE SUSHI

7

MARIA RAFTERY
ZUNI

8

CAITLIN RUTH
DEASY'S HARBOUR BAR

9

MICKAEL VILJANEN
GREGAN'S CASTLE

10

JUNICHI YOSHIYAGAWA
KAPPA-YA

THE HOUSE

Karl Dillon & Ian Connolly
4 Main Street
Howth, County Dublin
+353 (0) 1-839 6388
www.thehouse-howth.ie
info@thehouse-howth.ie

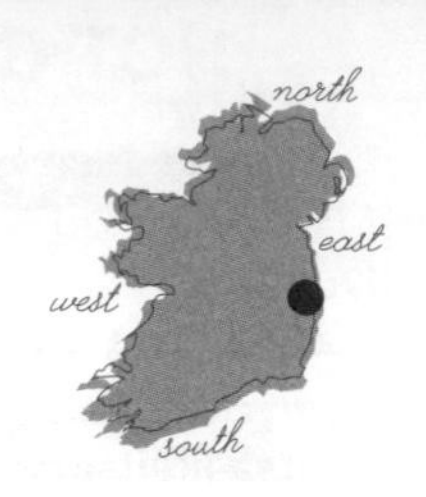

Karl Dillon and Ian Connolly's The House is just the sort of cracking value destination we need, says Caroline Byrne, a place for everyone, anytime.

So, how does this sound, for Tuesday night's dinner, for a mere tenner, in The House: "Poached smoked haddock, caramelised onion mash, sauté spinach, beurre blanc". If there is a better bargain in County Dublin, never mind in Howth, than this lovely, moreish dish, then we are bananas. Karl Dillon and Ian Connolly are doing what the people want, as well as doing what the people need in recessionary times, in their all-day café-restaurant-deli, and even if you do want to push the boat out a little, then dinner prices here are still amongst the best you will find. Virtually everything on the dinner menu is under and around twenty euro for main courses, and only the grilled rib-eye with horseradish mash goes for a few euro more. But it's not just good value: it's also extremely good cooking, smart, modern food that pushes all the right savoury notes: Guinness braised daube of beef; ray wing with sauté potatoes; chicken and apple sausage with apple and cider gravy; rice pudding with plum compote. Lovely.

● **OPEN:** 8.45am-5pm Mon, 8.45am-9.30pm Tue-Thu, 8.45am-10.30pm Fri, 10am-10.30pm Sat, 10am-9.30pm Sun
● **PRICE:** Lunch €10-€20, Dinner €30-€40
● **CREDIT CARDS:** Visa, Mastercard, Laser, Amex

● **NOTES:**
Wheelchair access. Surprise dinner for a Tenner Tue-Thu. Early bird €29.92-€24.95

● **DIRECTIONS:**
In the centre of Howth village.

ITSA4

Domini & Peaches Kemp
6A Sandymount Green
Dublin 4
+353 (0) 1-219 4676
www.itsabagel.com
itsa4@itsabagel.ie

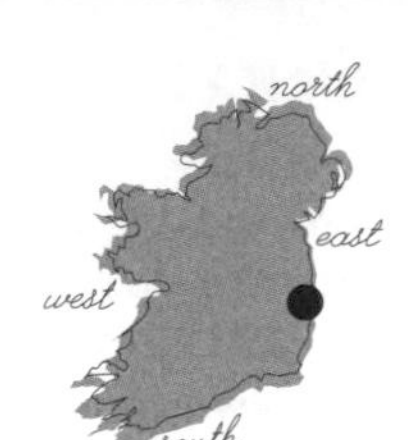

Sisters, sisters, there were never such smart sisters as Domini and Peaches Kemp, and their wit and discipline makes itsa4 a great dining address.

Quite how the Kemp sisters, Domini and Peaches, manage all the food businesses they currently run, in addition to writing journalism and writing cookery books and having families and whathaveyou, we simply do not know. We do know that they are formidable women, extremely disciplined and extremely hard-working, but in truth they behave like modern Super-women, multitasking to beat the band.

From all their enterprises, it is itsa4, a neat, handsome room in neat, handsome Sandymount Green, that rings our favourite bell. The food is impeccably sourced and cooked with flair, but it's also food that is winningly unpretentious, and that may be the secret of the Kemp girls' success: they have no egos; they just want to do their best, and their best is sure good enough for us. So, let's start with the Clogherhead crab salad, then roast chicken with champ, and then some lovely Goldenhill ice cream from Wicklow. The wine list is a cat-walk of great, great bottles, and the service is smart, calm and, again, unpretentious. itsalovelyplace.

- **OPEN:** noon-2pm Wed-Fri, 6pm-9pm Tue-Wed, 6pm-10pm Thu & Sat, 11am-3pm Sat, noon-3.30pm, 5.30pm-8pm Sun
- **PRICE:** Lunch & Dinner from €20-€35
- **CREDIT CARDS:** Visa, Mastercard, Laser

● NOTES:

Wheelchair access. Open Bank Holiday Mondays from noon. Children's menu.

● DIRECTIONS:

Overlooking Sandymount Green.

JUNO'S

Juha Salo
26 Parkgate Street
Dublin 1
+353 (0) 1-670 9820
www.junoscafe.com
junoscafe@gmail.com

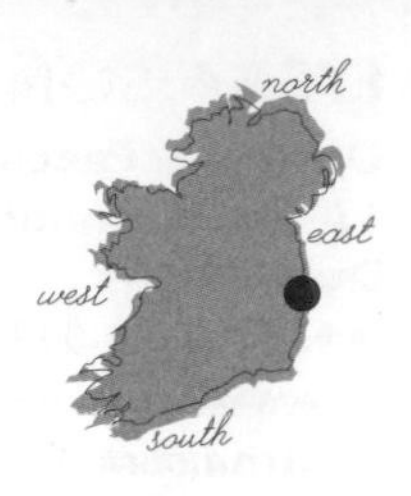

Caroline Byrne loves Juha Salo's zappy cooking, a taste of New York-diner style cooking in Dublin 1.

Juno's is a most unexpected and pleasant surprise, a gem tucked away in the less frequented neighbourhood of Parkgate Street. Think of a New York diner, like Zabaar's, only Irish, distinguished by quality Irish ingredients and the wholesome carby-ness of Irish cooking. The owners have managed to make something funky and appealing out of this narrow, unusually situated space, and the easy friendly manner of the staff will leave you happy to linger on as though you were hanging out in Manhattan and not one of Dublin city's less well-tended corners. The food is simple and classic: dressed home-smoked organic salmon on house brown bread; beetroot and Ryefield goat cheese salad with walnuts and croutons; air-dried Connemara ham with pickled fennel, dressed rocket and olives; or the 'roast roll of the day,' including the likes of corned beef with sauerkraut and pickles. In Juno's, the flavours are vibrant and perfectly balanced while meats melt in the mouth. Excellent fishcakes, great home fries, and their puds, such as lemon polenta and almond cake, are really on the money. Juha Salo has made a great start! CB

● **OPEN:** 8am-noon Mon-Fri, 10am-4pm Sat & Sun, noon-3pm Mon-Fri, 5pm-9.30pm Tue-Sat
● **PRICE:** Lunch €12, Dinner €25
● **CREDIT CARDS:** Visa, Mastercard, Laser

● **NOTES:**
Wheelchair access. Special lunch sitting Fridays, 4pm

● **DIRECTIONS:**
Just north of the River Liffey, just behond Wolfe Tone Quay, two minutes from Heuston Station.

LA MAISON

Olivier Quenet
15 Castle Market
Dublin 2
+353 (0) 1-672 7258
www.lamaisonrestaurant.ie
lamaison@live.ie

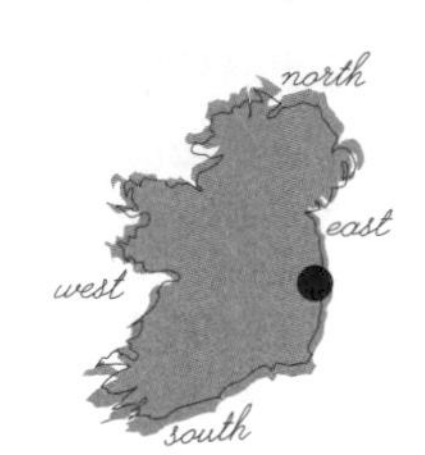

Olivier Quenet's classy, classic French food in a classy, classic French-style space rings all the bells. La Maison is polished, professional, pristine.

Olivier Quenet has just taken over the care of the cooking at The Schoolhouse on Northumberland Road in Dublin 4, having also run destinations in different parts of Dublin 4 and Dublin 6 over the last few years, but it's his smart city-centre room that is our favourite. He is a Breton born guy, and the food of France courses in his veins and his brain, which means it's very nice to see someone cooking carrots Vichy, and duck breast with bean cassoulet, and fillet steak tartare, and red mullet in pastry, and foie gras with Puy lentils. As Caroline Byrne has pointed out, M. Quenet knows exactly what a French restaurant is all about: he knows that the tablecloths and the napkins and the chairs and the artwork and the menu style and the service are all equally important elements along with the precision and execution of the food in creating an authentic, quintessential experience, and he pulls that off here in Castle Market with gas in the tank. The wine list is splendid, service is prompt and professional, and La Maison is a lovely room in which to meet a friend.

● **OPEN:** noon-3pm, 6pm-10pm Mon-Wed, noon-3pm, 6pm-11pm Thu & Fri, noon-11pm Sat, 1pm-9pm Sun
● **PRICE:** Meals €35-€40
● **CREDIT CARDS:** Visa, Mastercard, Laser

● **NOTES:**
Wheelchair access.

● **DIRECTIONS:**
Behind the Powerscourt Townhouse Centre, just off Grafton Street.

MANIFESTO

Lucio Paduano & Eugenio Massitelli
208 Rathmines Road
Dublin 6
+353 (0) 1-496 8096
www.manifestorestaurant.ie
manifestorestaurant@gmail.com

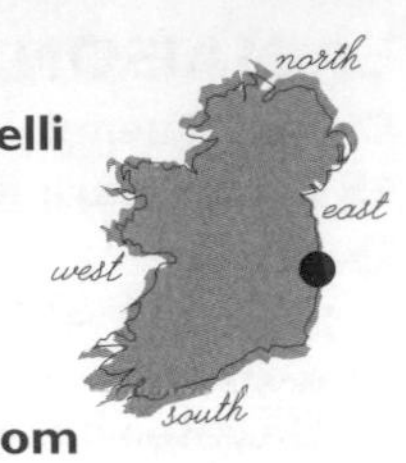

CB loves the "local restaurant done right" simplicity of Manifesto, not to mention the pizzas and pasta.

Manifesto is a simple establishment, friendly and informal, filled with locals and plenty of Italians at that. On walking through the door you're greeted by the warmth of the staff as much as of the large wood fire oven that occupies the front of the restaurant, and wave after wave of glorious Italian aromas from both oven and kitchen to the rear. Around you, great frisbee-like pizzas whir by, their thin, crispy bases generously topped with Parma ham and torn buffalo mozzarella, such as the 'Mamy' (tomato sauce, grated mozzarella, aubergine, Parma ham, Parmesan, topped with fresh buffalo mozzarella), or fine bresaola and rocket, as on the Carpaccio (mozzarella topped with bresaola, rocket, Parmesan shavings, lemon juice and black pepper). Don't miss the spaghetti alla chitarra all'astice, where sweet lobster meets superb fresh pasta, or the tagliata di mazo, a rib-eye steak served with rocket. The wine list is concise and affordable, value for money is extra-keen, even with ingredients like lobster. Manifesto is a local place done right. CB.

- **OPEN:** 5pm-11pm Mon-Sun
- **PRICE:** Dinner €35
- **CREDIT CARDS:** Visa, Mastercard, Laser

- **NOTES:**

Wheelchair access.

- **DIRECTIONS:**

On the main street of Rathmines, which is south of the city centre.

MICHIE SUSHI

Michel Piare & Anna van Excel
11 Chelmsford Lane, Ranelagh
Dublin 6
+353 (0) 1-497 6438
www.michiesushi.com
info@michiesushi.com

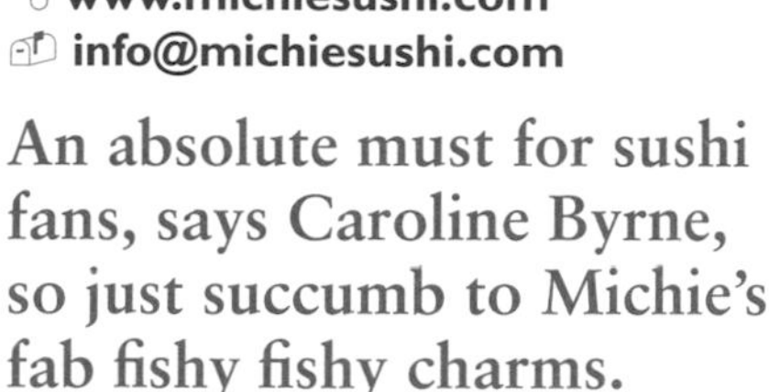

An absolute must for sushi fans, says Caroline Byrne, so just succumb to Michie's fab fishy fishy charms.

This is the best sushi restaurant in Dublin. You may have trouble finding the modest little nook, hidden down a lane off the main strip in Ranelagh, but this adds to its charm. And you're certainly rewarded for your efforts: hell, it'd be worth the schlep if they were way out in the sticks: it's that good. Depending on what owner-chef Michel Piare puts up for the day's sashimi special, raw fish lovers could be anywhere between heaven and even more heaven. One day it's butter soft beautiful tranches of swordfish, another (if you're lucky) it's gleaming sea urchin, melt in the mouth and fresh as the sea. Everything that passes your lips is breathtakingly fresh and full of vibrant flavour, which is the simple beauty of good sushi. Michel's inventive special rolls are delicious too, particularly the soft shell crab roll, made with spring onion, flying fish roe and avocado. Non-fish needs are also catered for, with popular choices such as chicken yakitori, a tasty side of chicken on skewers, or hot dishes like vegetable yaki soba. Service, managed by Michel's wife Anna, is great.

- **OPEN:** noon-10pm Tue-Sun
- **PRICE:** Bento Lunch €8.90, Sushi combos €9-€12.50
- **CREDIT CARDS:** Visa, Mastercard, Laser

- **NOTES:**

Wheelchair access. Catering menu available. Eatout and delivery menu. Delivery, day and evening, in the local area. Minimum order for delivery €15.

- **DIRECTIONS:**

Just off the main Ranelagh, Sandford Road interchange.

NONNA VALENTINA

Stefano Crescenzi & Eileen Dunne
1-2 Portobello Road
Dublin 6
+353 (0) 1-454 9866
www.nonnavalentina.ie
dunneandcrescenzi@hotmail.com

"Two stressed people entered the restaurant. Two happy and sated people left." That's Leslie Williams' joyous take on Nonna Valentina's fine food.

"A lovely bright room, pristine tablecloths and settings, scrubbed floorboards and friendly staff." Ah, isn't the way Leslie Williams describes the first impressions of Nonna Valentina just exactly the way you want a classic Italian restaurant to look and feel? Everything in its right place, so bring on the food: "Bruschetta is toasted, garlic-rubbed Nonna's bread with lots of chopped sweet tomato: a perfect appetite whetter. The fresh mushroom and truffle ravioli with salted butter and Parmigiano jus offers fresh silky pasta with rich Parmesan aromas and flavours: delicious. Red cabbage and wine risotto came with strips of deep-fried red cabbage on top, unctuous and quite soft carnaroli rice, this was very rich, with the cabbage adding both sweetness and a touch of umami, and the red wine jus smeared around the plate was a delicious, bitter little kick. Very good. A carafe of house wine is a light cabernet from the North East" And that's the Nonna Valentina formula for taking two stressed out people, and turning them into happy bunnies, via the gift of great, precise, smart Italian cooking.

- **OPEN:** 6pm-late Tue-Fri, noon-late Sat & Sun
- **PRICE:** Sun Lunch €22.50, Dinner from €30
- **CREDIT CARDS:** All major cards accepted

● NOTES:

Full wheelchair access. Credit cards accepted, but no cheques.

● DIRECTIONS:

On the banks of the canal in between the Portobello and Harold's Cross bridges.

O'CONNELL'S

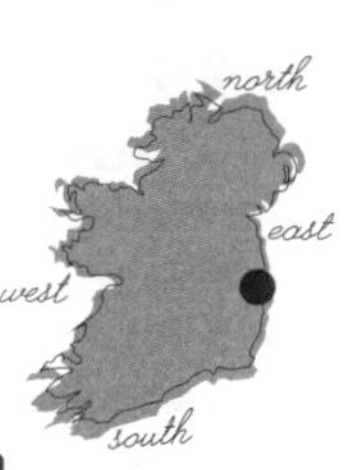

Tom O'Connell
133/135 Morehampton Road
Donnybrook, Dublin 4
+353 (0) 1-665 5940
www.oconnellsdonnybrook.com
info@oconnellsdonnybrook.com

Two great Laois talents fuse together to bring the old and the new to Donnybrook: O'Connell's is hot.

Two great, original County Laois food talents – restaurateur Tom O'Connell and chef Lorcan Cribbin – combine with manager Giorgio Cappiello to create the best thing to have hit D4 since Roly's opened back in 1992. O'Connell's, writes Caroline Byrne, is interesting in every way, and a great arrival for Donnybrook. The wine list is fascinating and original, the menu offer is framed to house great value offers, and the cooking is right on the money: black pudding, veal sweetbreads, foie gras and wild mushroom sausage; roast cod with scampi and artichoke Provençale; venison with poached pears, celeriac truffle and madeira; Cullohill apple tart with Gathabawn ice cream. Mr Cribbin's touch in the kitchen is sure, and right from the day they opened the doors in Mid-November, the service was assured, polite and engaged. The brasserie-style room in what used to be Madigan's pub works a treat. More importantly, Mr Cribbin's modern food with Mr O'Connell's old-style service is a unique combination. Together they have forged something with true appeal.

- **OPEN:** 11am-10pm Tue-Sun
- **PRICE:** Lunch €15, Dinner from €30
- **CREDIT CARDS:** All major cards accepted

NOTES:

Full wheelchair access. Open for morning coffee and fresh bakery weekdays, breakfast on Sundays.

DIRECTIONS:

Located at the first major junction in Donnybrook, when approaching from the South.

ONE PICO

Eamonn O'Reilly
5-6 Molesworth Place
Schoolhouse Lane, Dublin 2
+ 353 (0) 1-676 0200
www.onepico.com
one_pico@yahoo.ie

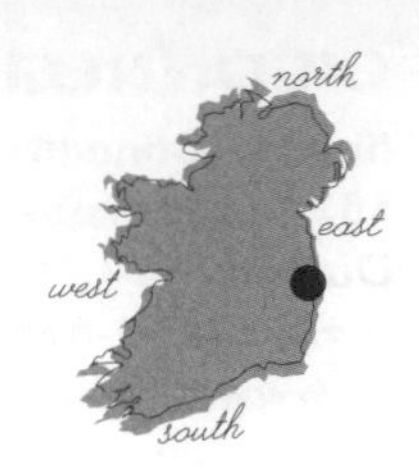

One Pico is bang on the money these days, with chef-patron Eamonn O'Reilly right on top of his game, sending out great Irish cooking.

One of the mantras of Bridgetone editor Caroline Byrne is that when Irish restaurateurs do what they know how to do, then they are amongst the very best in the world. One of the Dublin chefs who best proves this is Eamonn O'Reilly of the handsome, hip and successful One Pico. A few years back, O'Reilly expanded his business empire – he still also runs Bleu Bistro just around the corner – and it did him no favours. Then he started to experiment with fusion and molecular cooking, and it did him no favours. Today, he just concentrates on sending out the food he loves to cook, served in a beautiful room at some of the best-value prices in the city, and it shows him at his proud best, and it shows him as one of the best, a seriously talented, hard-working chef who has rediscovered the thrill of running a great city restaurant. Stick with his classic dishes – ham hock terrine; foie gras parfait; perfectly judged fish cookery; superb desserts and some of the best petits fours – and you will find delight in a restaurant serviced by a kitchen that doesn't put a foot wrong.

- **OPEN:** noon-11.30pm Mon-Sun
- **PRICE:** Lunch €25, Dinner €49
- **CREDIT CARDS:** Visa, Mastercard, Laser, Amex

- **NOTES:**

Limited wheelchair access. Pre-theatre dinner €25

- **DIRECTIONS:**

On the corner of a small laneway – Molesworth Place – which runs between Dawson Street and Kildare Street.

101 TALBOT

Neal & Jenny Magee
101 Talbot Street
Dublin 1
+353 (0) 1-874 5011
www.101talbot.ie

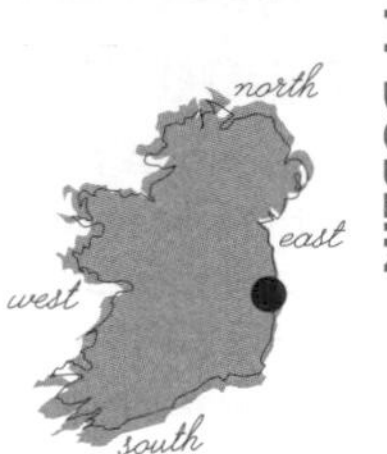

Quality; integrity; energy; authenticity. Oh, and it's also weird and wonderful, says Elizabeth Field of the iconic 101 Talbot restaurant, a Dublin classic.

"The food has quality and integrity" is how Elizabeth Field sees Neal Magee's cooking in 101 Talbot. And whilst that is true, it is of course only one element of the attractiveness of this city-centre institution. What else, Liz? "The early bird dinner at €21.50 is a steal". Well, that's for sure: 101 has always delivered incredible bangs per buck. Is there more? Of course there is: "The place was buzzing with Thursday evening shoppers and just about everyone else. No empty tables in the house." And there you have it: 101 isn't just a restaurant. It's a hub for food, for being sociable, for enjoying wines, for getting the mainline of the city centre. Sit down in here, and you feel you are at the centre of the planet. What did you eat, Liz? Cumin and cinnamon-tinged carrot soup; potato rosti with Crozier Blue cheese, sautéed greens, onion marmalade and thyme cream sauce; char-grilled lamb steak marinated with yogurt, chilli and garlic, with sweet potato wedges, chilli sauce and raita. "Energy, authenticity, weird and wonderful, I hope it never changes." Us too.

- **OPEN:** noon-3pm, 5pm-11pm Tue-Sat
- **PRICE:** Dinner €35
- **CREDIT CARDS:** All major cards accepted

● NOTES:

Reservations recommended at weekends. Recommended for vegetarians. Early bird, 5pm-7.30pm €21.95. No wheelchair access.

● DIRECTIONS:

3 minutes' walk from the Dublin Spire.

PEARL BRASSERIE

Sebastian Masi & Kirsten Batt
20 Merrion Street Upper
Dublin 2
+353 (0) 1-661 3572
www.pearl-brasserie.com
info@pearl-brasserie.com

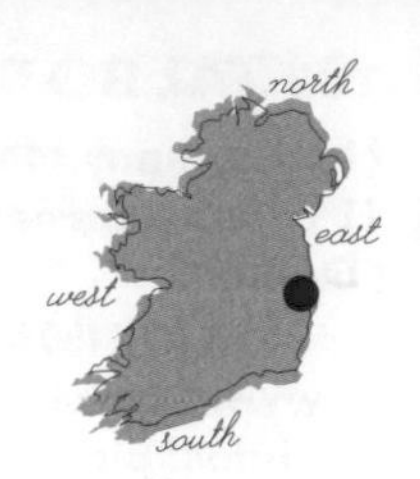

With a second brasserie – Locks – just opened in Portobello, Sebastian and Kirsten are showing that smart food at good prices can beat the recession.

Sebastian and Kirsten aren't letting a little recession stand in their way, and in addition to their hot and happening brasserie, Pearl, they have newly opened another brasserie, Locks, in Portobello, where Rory Carvill is heading up the kitchen, having made the move from working in L'Ecrivain alongside Derry Clarke. Back in Upper Merrion Street, they have enjoyed ten successful years, built on the twin pillars of Mr Masi's food and Ms Batt's service. The cooking is clean, logical and spot-on, centred on classic dishes – foie gras with brioche; Pata Negra ham with Comté; Caesar salad; oysters with shallot vinaigrette – but there are lots of nice surprises going on with every plate, like Dublin Bay prawns with veal brisket, or remoulade with fillet and cheek of beef, or crispy oxtail with a ham-hock risotto. Caroline Byrne has described Mr Masi's food as "quietly outstanding", and so it is, so expect to be impressed. Pearl is great value for money, the room is quite lovely, and can be very hard to leave, especially after a glass or two at lunchtime. Cancel the day!

- **OPEN:** noon-2.30pm Mon-Fri, 6pm-10.30pm Mon-Sat
- **PRICE:** Lunch €22-€35, Dinner €55-€60
- **CREDIT CARDS:** All major cards accepted

● NOTES:

Wheelchair access. Minis menu served in cocktail bar. Recommended for vegetarians.

● DIRECTIONS:

Opposite the Government Buildings on Merrion Street.

PICHET

Stephen Gibson & Nick Munier
14-15 Trinity Street
Dublin 2
+353 (0) 1-667 1060
www.pichetrestaurant.com
info@pichetrestaurant.com

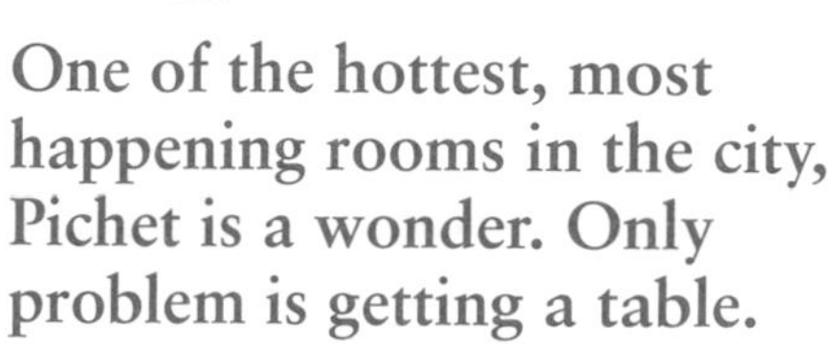

One of the hottest, most happening rooms in the city, Pichet is a wonder. Only problem is getting a table.

"We want to make simple good food that's cooked well", Stephen Gibson told *The Boston Globe*. What a modest, sensible and wise philosophy for a chef-patron, especially when you consider that so many chefs are neither modest, sensible nor wise. But, then, everything about Pichet and its core team – f-o-hs Nick and Denise Munier and pastry chef Natasha McGowan, along with chef Gibson – is different. They had their act tuned and tweaked from the moment they opened their doors, and acclaim was instant: the only problem with Pichet is getting a table. Mr Gibson's food is as smart as it gets, robust yet refined, with big flavours counterpointed by bullet points from ingredients such as wasabi, harissa, basil, watercress and saffron. It all eats well: crab with chorizo aioli and clams à la Grecque; cod with shellfish orzo and roast scallop; pork with caper and spinach cream; shorthorn beef with bearnaise and fries; chocolate brownie with stout ice cream. Mr Munier's wine list is as imperiously confident as his service, and Pichet ticks every box. Twice.

- **OPEN:** 8am-4pm Mon-Fri, 10am-4pm Sat, noon-4pm Sun in the Cafe. noon-3pm, 5pm-10.30pm Mon-Sat, noon-3pm, 5pm-9pm Sun in the Restaurant.
- **PRICE:** Lunch €20-€25, Dinner €40
- **CREDIT CARDS:** All major cards accepted

NOTES:
Wheelchair access.

DIRECTIONS:
Trinity Street runs off Dame Street, just near the Central Bank.

GREAT SIGNATURE DISHES

1

Salad of wood pigeon, hazelnut purée, poached cherries – No 1 Pery Square

2

Slow-roasted salmon, dilisk emulsion – Shu

3

Prawn risotto with tomato, basil, langoustine butter – Mourne Seafood Bar

4

Smoked beef with wild coltsfoot – The Strawberry Tree

5

Kettyle chicken with mushroom froth – Viewmount House

6

Sirloin with oxtail potato cake – The Cottage

7

Crubeen with pickled ox tongue, black pudding soup – The Brown Bear

8

Black sesame ice cream, tempura of banana – Kappa-Ya

9

Quail with Szechuan pepper – Thornton's

10

Spicy Ma Po tofu – China Sichuan

THE PORT HOUSE

Lee Sim
64a South William Street
Dublin 2
+ 353 (0) 1-677 0298
www.porthouse.ie
info@porthouse.ie

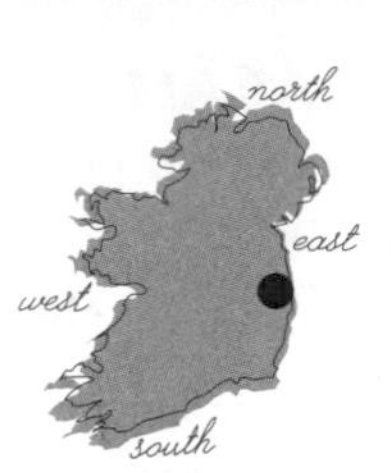

A little slice of San Sebastian in central Dublin and a fun place to be. The drinks are exceptional.

The Port House is fun. Caroline Byrne, Leslie Williams and John McKenna of the Bridgestone parish found themselves together in here late one summer evening in 2010, and after a lot of umming and aaahing they decided that they would have the patatas mojo as well as the patatas alïoli. And they had the pulpo al Gallega, and a plate of Iberian ham. And sure with the night that was in it they also had the gambas al pil pil, and the chanquettes, those lovely deep-fried whitebait with salt and lemon, and the frango piri piri, those lip-smacking chicken wings. And with 80 wines, sherries and ports from Iberia to choose, sure they had to have a drop of the Txakolina from Ameztoi and the Olvena Crianza. And it was all just delightful: a superbly atmospheric room that takes you right back to wherever and whenever you last had plates of tapas and glasses of hard cider when in Spain itself, all winking lights and a cave-like interior. They enjoyed good, friendly service from Hubert, and the three agreed that, really, this sort of outfit is just pure Bridgestone. And Bridgestone editors don't usually agree. Consensus!

- **OPEN:** 11.30am-11.30pm Mon-Fri & Sat, 12.30pm-midnight Sat
- **PRICE:** Tapas and Pintxos €3-€15
- **CREDIT CARDS:** Visa, Mastercard, Laser, Amex

● NOTES:
Limited wheelchair access. Cold Pintxos available at the bar all day, every day.

● DIRECTIONS:
South William Street is in the area just behind Grafton Street, near St Stephen's Green.

RASAM

Nisheeth Tak
Eagle Pub, 18/19 Glasthule Road
Glasthule, County Dublin
+353 (0) 1-230 0600
www.rasam.ie
info@rasam.ie

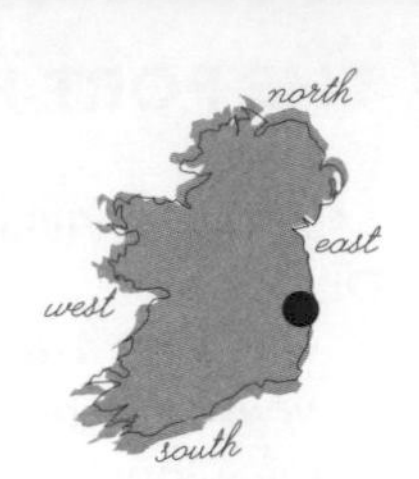

Rasam's authenticity and stellar levels of execution means it stays on top of the ethnic pile in Ireland.

Nisheeth Tak's restaurant can be summarised in one phrase: the critic's choice. "I have loved this restaurant since it opened seven years ago", confessed Catherine Cleary in *The Irish Times*, whilst Ernie Whalley once said that Rasam was "Up there with the best Irish restaurants". We agree. Nisheeth Tak's achievement in Rasam is enormous, and he created the template of a gorgeous room and serious, echt ethnic cuisine long before anyone else thought of it. Where other ethnic food takes shortcuts, chef Sanjay Vishwakarma and his team put in the effort; the sheer variety of flavours, seasoning and styles in the dishes which are drawn from all over the sub-continent is breathtaking, but equally breathtaking is the finesse visited on every detail, from the naan bread flecked with toasted coconut and plump raisins to the deep-fried yogurt patties to their signature dish of lal maas, lamb cooked on the bone with chillies, ginger, coriander, tomatoes and garam masala. Beautiful food, beautiful room and, for once, the critics are united!

- **OPEN:** 5.30pm-11pm Mon-Sun
- **PRICE:** Dinner €45
- **CREDIT CARDS:** Visa, Mastercard, Laser

NOTES:
Early bird menu, 5.30pm-7pm Sun-Thur, €19.95-€23.95. No wheelchair access.

DIRECTIONS:
Over the Eagle House in the centre of Glasthule. GPS 53.286667 -6.123056Winding

SABA

Paul Cadden
26-28 Clarendon Street
Dublin 2
+353 (0) 1-679 2000
www.sabadublin.com
feedback@sabadublin.com

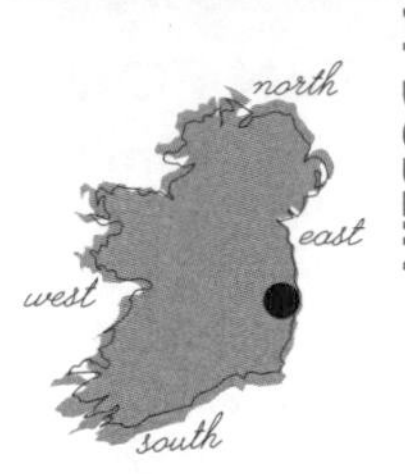

Paul Cadden's super stylish Saba is a Sanuk kind of place: great fun, and with great, echt ethnic cooking.

Paul Cadden is a dynamic young guy, and with chef Taweesak Trakoolwattana he has fashioned one of the city's best ethnic restaurants in Saba, both in terms of exciting Thai and Vietnamese cooking, and also in terms of its exuberant, playful decor and sexy, tongue-in-cheek ambience. It's the sort of space you might find in the glossy pages of the weekend *Financial Times*, complete with an audience who look like they hang out with David Collins and John Rocha. It's a fun place, even before you have one of their wicked cocktails. Any time of day, we are game ball for their signature Saba dishes, such as soft-shelled crab, or the hake in banana leaf with red curry sauce, or the steamed seabass with pickled plum and ginger, and the dishes are wonderfully chilli-clean and vibrant, enlivening and stimulating, and whilst the menu is extensive, the care and attention lavished on each dish is reassuring and makes for reliable, consistent eating. The room works best when you are with a bunch of people, in which case the intoxication of this zesty, chilli-rich food soon leads to intoxication of another sort. Let tomorrow sort itself.

- **OPEN:** noon-late Mon-Sun
- **PRICE:** Lunch €15.95-€19.95, Dinner €25-€30
- **CREDIT CARDS:** Visa, Mastercard, Laser, Amex

NOTES:

Wheelchair access from Balfe Street, next to the Westbury Hotel. Saba to Go, (takeout and foodstore) 13 Rathgar Rd, D6. Tel 01-406 0200

DIRECTIONS:

Clarendon Street runs parallel to Grafton Street, the main shopping street of central Dublin.

TEN FOURTEEN CLONTARF

Gareth Smith
324 Clontarf Road
Dublin 3
+353 (0) 1-230 0600
www.restaurant1014.com
margaretbutler1014@gmail.com

north
east
west
south

Gareth Smith and his crew are getting everything right in 1014, says Caroline Byrne, and it's a local treasure and an essential neighbourhood star.

1014 is owned by the charity CASA (Caring and Sharing Association), which provides a support network for people with disabilities, so eating here serves two good causes. The first is that you help to support CASA. The second is that you support the cause of good food, sourced smartly and cooked with care and passion, served charmingly and unpretentiously. In just a couple of years, Gareth Smith's cooking has won unanimous acclaim, and certain signature dishes – their brilliant chowder; roast scallops with sesame and ginger; cod and chips in beer batter; haddock gratin with cheddar cheese and bread crumb crust – have all become firm favourites for a devoted local audience. We also love the neighbourhood feel of 1014, a restaurant by the locals for the locals, and there isn't a happier dining room on the Northside. So let's meet for Sunday lunch, enjoy ballotine of chicken and Jane Russell's black pudding, then sirloin of Kilbeggan beef and mash, with a Clontarf salad, and then a walk along the waterfront. Perfect.

- **OPEN:** 10.30am-9pm Mon-Wed, 10.30am-10pm Thu-Sat, 12.30pm-8.30pm Sun
- **PRICE:** Lunch Main €9-€13, Dinner €25-€35
- **CREDIT CARDS:** Visa, Mastercard, Laser

● NOTES:
Disabled access. Early Bird menu €19.95-€24.95

● DIRECTIONS:
Opposite the Wooden Bridge @ 324 Clontarf Road.

THORNTON'S

Kevin & Muriel Thornton
St. Stephen's Green
Dublin 2
+353 (0) 1-478 7008
www.thorntonsrestaurant.com
thorntonsrestaurant@eircom.net

north
east
west
south
hot

Kevin Thornton and his team are cooking the food of their life right now, every dish a challenge and a triumph.

Kevin Thornton is back on a roll, producing food of world-class standards, and doing so day in, day out, at keen and affordable prices. Tony and his wife, "steadily working our way through your places to stay and places to eat", wrote to say that a dinner in Thornton's "was the best meal we have ever eaten in Ireland. This was a level of food and service well above anything we have experienced, and the vegetarian menu was simply world class". Bridgestone editor Elizabeth Field, back in Ireland for a trip, concurs about the new level Thornton's has moved to: "There is nothing extraneous in the cooking, presentation or service. This is a really tight ship, and a very 'grown up' place to eat because Kevin's take on Irish food is at once intellectual and artistic, as well as technically superb." Elizabeth enjoyed mussels in saffron consommé; quail with Szechaun pepper; Atlantic sea bream with baby artichokes; guinea fowl with Savoy cabbage and carrots, and a pitch-perfect cheese plate. Kevin Thornton and his team are right back bang on target, as good as ever.

- **OPEN:** 6pm-9.30pm (last orders) Tue-Sat, 12.30pm-1pm (last orders) Thur-Sat.
- **PRICE:** Lunch €25, Dinner €79-€125
- **CREDIT CARDS:** All major cards accepted

NOTES:
Full wheelchair access. Recommended for vegetarians. Pre-theatre €49

DIRECTIONS:
On the west side of St Stephen's Green.

THE WINDING STAIR

Elaine Murphy
40 Lower Ormond Quay
Dublin 1
+353 (0) 1-872 7320
www.winding-stair.com
restaurant@winding-stair.com

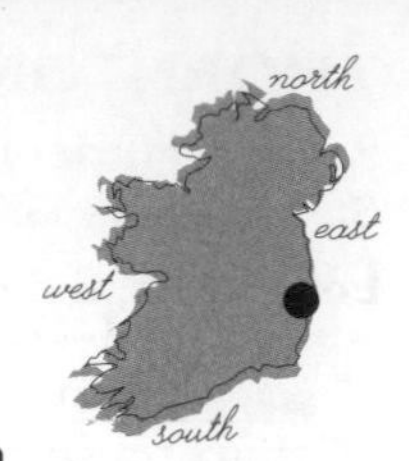

Recession? No one has told the punters and staff in TWS, a restaurant that surges with electrifying energy and brio.

Nobody writes better menus than Elaine Murphy and her crew in TWS. If you asked us how to write a menu, we would simply hand you a copy of the one we enjoyed one lunchtime in August 2010 when we met some friends, and say: "You write a menu like this". The descriptions of the dishes and the principal producers whose work inspires them is nothing less than perfect. And guess what? The menus are good to read, for sure. And good to think, which is essential. But, they are even better to eat, from Ted Browne's Kerry prawns on toast to McLoughlin's spring lamb to O'Doherty's black pig pork neck to Nicholson's hand-smoked haddock. Everything is so ruddy, so real, so elemental, so satisfying and enlivening that it takes us right back to one of our favourite food quotes, from the great Wendell Berry, who said in 1989 that, "Eating is an agricultural act". Eating in TWS is an agricultural and culinary triumph, and this restaurant is not just one of Ireland's best restaurants, it is also one of Ireland's most important places to eat.

- **OPEN:** noon-5pm Sun-Thur, noon-3pm Fri & Sat, 5.30pm-11pm Mon-Sun
- **PRICE:** Lunch €17-€22.95, Dinner €40
- **CREDIT CARDS:** Visa, Mastercard

- **NOTES:** No wheelchair access. Pre-theatre menu €24-€29.95. Private dining room.

- **DIRECTIONS:**

North side of the River Liffey, beside Ha'penny Bridge. GPS 53.346580 -6.263626

ARD BIA @ NIMMO'S

Aoibheann McNamara
Spanish Arch
Long Walk, Galway
+353 (0) 91-561 114
www.ardbia.com
ardbia@gmail.com

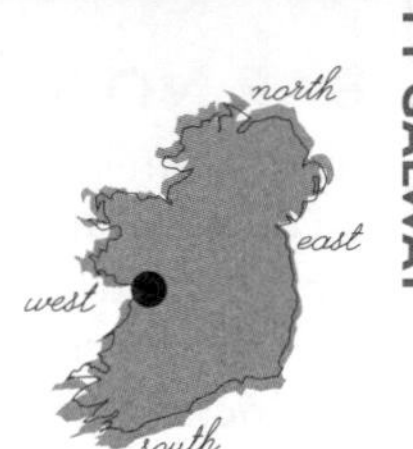

Fuse two great Galway institutions and you get a unique restaurant persona – Ard Bia and Nimmo's in one, thanks to the dynamic Aoibheann McNamara.

Until Aoibheann McNamara came along, the person who put the greatest style into using the endearment "darling" was the great Bunny Wailer. "I'll play your fav'rit' song, daarrlingg, so we can rock it all night long, daaarrrlinggg, yeah, yeah", he sang on the classic "Mellow Mood" from "Bunny Wailer Sings The Wailers". But Ms McNamara can out-do Bunny when it comes to turning "darling" into the word that speaks straight, directly, unmistakably, just and only to you. "Good evening, darling" she says as you walk into the cloisters of Ard Bia @ Nimmo's, and she has you straight away. No contest. You just turned into a little puppy. Aoibheann is a great host and she runs a great downstairs café and a great upstairs restaurant, with food unlike anyone else's. Niamh Fox's cooking is vibrant, tactile and fresh, as well as surprising – sea trout with smoked pork; striploin with wild mushroom batter; pearl barley risotto with St Tola goats' curd. It's exactly the right food in the right room with the right, languid, laissez-faire, laid-back philosophy. Only in Galway, darling.

- **OPEN:** Cafe open 9am-3.30pm, Restaurant open 6pm-10pm
- **PRICE:** Dinner €38, Cafe Lunch €6-€12
- **CREDIT CARDS:** Visa, Mastercard, Laser, Amex

● NOTES:

Wheelchair access, but no disabled toilet in Nimmos. Rotating exhibitions. Ard Bia Cookery courses & Art Gallery. Early menu €24-€28

● DIRECTIONS:

Down by the River Corrib, under the arch across from new museum.

BAR NO 8

Jessica Murphy, Tom Sheridan
8 Dock Road, Galway
County Galway
+353 (0) 91-565111
dockeight@gmail.com
www.bar8.ie

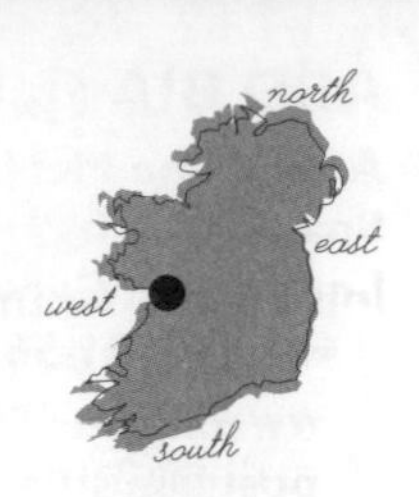

Jess Murphy's rigorous cooking & ethical sourcing has conjured up some of the best Galway food.

No question but that Jess Murphy's cooking has caught the zeitgeist in Galway. The informal setting of Tom Sheridan's funky pub and the zestful, spontaneous nature of Ms Murphy's food have allied to make a gastropub that is neither pub nor restaurant but some manner of idealised halfway house with cracking cooking. In that Kiwi style which so values the freshness of quotidian things, Ms Murphy loves beetroots, and dandelion leaves, haddock and crab, Mayo hill lamb and smashing poultry from Galway's iconic Friendly Farmer. This is cooking with chutzpah, and it is particularly interesting that Ms Murphy is a vegetarian who nevertheless cooks meat for her customers, a measure of her discipline as well as her intellect. She sources from the best folk in the west, giving the food an important ethical as well as local nature, and everything, from the menu name-checking to the funky room to the Coolattin cheddar served with rye fruit cake simply works. A glass or several of Galway Hooker, a trawl through the light bites, the bigger bites, the after 8's, it's all so fine.

- **OPEN:** 4.30pm-11pm Mon-Thu, 12.30pm-11.30pm Fri-Sun
- **PRICE:** Lunch €15, Dinner €30
- **CREDIT CARDS:** Visa, Mastercard, Laser

● NOTES:
Wheelchair access.

● DIRECTIONS:
Down at the dock area of Galway city.

INIS MEÁIN RESTAURANT & SUITES

Ruairí & Marie-Therese de Blácam
Inis Meain, Aran Islands
+353 (0) 86-826 6026
www.inismeain.com
post@inismeain.com

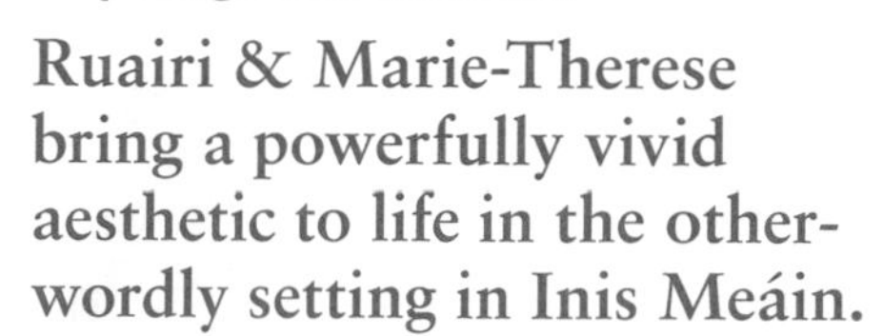

Ruairi & Marie-Therese bring a powerfully vivid aesthetic to life in the other-wordly setting in Inis Meáin.

Ruairí and Marie-Therese de Blácam are one of those duos whose combined skills are not simply amplified by each other, they are in fact magnified by each other. His classicism is counterpointed by her iconoclasm, his island introversion is congratulated by her County Cork openness. As we have noted before, they are fortunate to have a shared aesthetic, in food, style, design, outlook, and it makes them a formidable team.So, step into this stunning room, with its jaw-dropping views out across Inis Meain, and be prepared to let this simple but disciplined food entrance you in the way in which the best cooking does. With vegetables and potatoes from their garden, with local fish and shellfish, they let the ingredients do the talking, and anyone familiar with the cooking of the great Johnnie Cooke will be right at home here for, like his mentor, Ruairi de Blacam's cooking is understated and classic: lobster salad with aioli; dressed crab; seafood pot with tomato and baby fennel; apple tart with crème anglaise. Book and get ready to be amazed.

- **OPEN:** Apr-Sept, dinner only
- **PRICE:** Dinner main courses €16-€35
- **CREDIT CARDS:** Visa, Mastercard, Laser

- **NOTES:** Take ferry from Rosaveal, or the plane from Inverin. Four large suite rooms, priced in special packages inclusive of dinner.

- **DIRECTIONS:**
In the middle of the island, pass the only pub on your right, take the next right, then look out for stone building 100m on your left.

KAPPA-YA

Junichi Yoshiyagawa
5 Middle Street
Galway
County Galway
+353 (0) 86-3543616
kappaya@eircom.net>

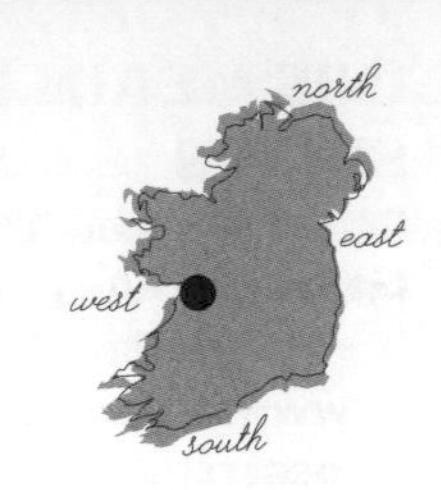

There is no cooking like the Kappa-ya Saturday night dinner, one of the most outrageous meals in the world.

"You've never seen the likes of the food served by chef Junichi Yoshiyagawa" wrote food writer Aoife Carrigy after a weekend dinner at Kappa-ya. Spot on, Aoife. If there is any manner of precedent for the lurid, surreal concoctions that Junichi invents, it might be Cork's brilliant iconoclast, Seamus O'Connell, of The Ivory Tower. But even Seamus would hardly think to serve "Galway Bay prawn cooked one second with burnt sesame oil", or "black sesame ice cream with tempura of banana", or to pair camembert ice cream with salted cherry blossom, aduki beans and green tea chiffon cake. This cooking is truly out of the box, except that it works, superbly, as if Junichi has worked out, in a culinary sense, that thesis + antithesis = synthesis. So, this isn't fusion cooking: this is synthesis cooking, and the Saturday night dinner will blow your mind. During the week, the food is more straight-ahead, but still superb. But those who want to walk on the wild side should book well head for Saturday night, order the good sake, and get blown away.

- **OPEN:** noon-4pm Mon-Fri, 1pm-6pm Sat, Cafe open 4pm-7pm, Dinner 7pm-9.30pm Tue-Fri. Sat pre-booked only, from 8pm
- **PRICE:** Lunch €11-€18, Dinner €16.50-€37
- **CREDIT CARDS:** Visa, Mastercard, Laser

● NOTES:
Wheelchair access, but no disabled toilet. Recommended for children.

● DIRECTIONS:
Middle Street is between High St and St. Augustine Pl.

OSCAR'S

Michael O'Meara & Sinead Hughes
Upper Dominick Street
Galway, County Galway
+353 (0) 91-582180
www.oscarsbistro.ie
oscarsgalway@eircom.net

Off to Oscar's to eat "Sweaty Betty"! Ha! Could there be a more Galway thing to do than that. And what is "Sweaty Betty"? Turn up and find out.

After ten years of happy cooking, Michael O'Meara and Sinead Hughes have shifted their beloved bistro sideways, focusing more on the fish and shellfish cookery that has become the major part of their food offer. So, Oscar's is now Oscar's Seafood Bistro, and on the menu – when it is available – you will indeed find "Sweaty Betty" or, to give it its correct name, Greater Forked Beard. You will also find Michael's spin on classics such as fish and chips – he uses a pakora batter, and favours Maris Piper potatoes for the fries; grilled Clare Island salmon; fishcakes in oatmeal crust; and specialities such as prawn and chilli sambale which reveal Michael's love of oriental flavours. But a large part of the menu is only decided on the day, depending on the fish offered to Michael by such stellar merchants as Gannet Fishmongers. That's how you run a proper seafood restaurant, and a proper seafood restaurant is what Galway has always needed. Mr O'Meara, when he isn't cheffing, is also a superb food photographer, and has just commenced an M.Sc in culinary arts. Phew!

- **OPEN:** 6.30pm-late Mon-Fri, 6pm-late Sat
- **PRICE:** Dinner €30-€40
- **CREDIT CARDS:** Visa, Mastercard, Laser

● NOTES:
Wheelchair access, but no disabled toilet. Early bird menu, €20

● DIRECTIONS:
Cross the bridge at Jury's, and follow the road past Monroe's Tavern, the restaurant is across the street from Roisin Dubh bar.

GLOBAL VILLAGE

Martin Bealin & Nuala Cassidy
Upper Main Street, Dingle
County Kerry
+353 (0) 66-915 2325
www.globalvillagedingle.com
admin@globalvillagedingle.com

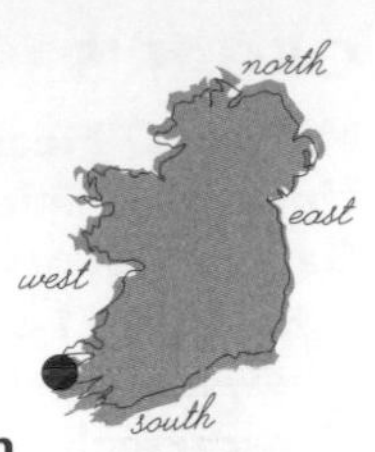

Marti & Nuala's restaurant is devoted to the local fish and meats of Dingle, and the cooking is spot on.

Global Village may be the sort of name for a restaurant that suggests that you will encounter a globalised cuisine hailing from all the corners of the earth. In fact, Martin Bealin and Nuala Cassidy's Global Village in Dingle is a food destination devoted to local foods, in particular inshore fish and local, sustainable meats, with the names of the farmers who rear the beef and lamb used actually written on the blackboard. It's a comfortable, white tablecloth room, with comfortable, hugely enjoyable cooking, from the selection of oysters – with blue cheese ice cream! – to the duck broth to the very fine fish cookery to the excellent beef served with rosti potatoes, which both Sam and PJ McKenna ordered as their main course and which both of them demolished in double-quick time. Plating is elegant and considered, with the dishes looking artful on large, square plates and with little white jugs used for sauces, but there is nothing stuffy about the room or the service, and all the McKennas had a thoroughly wonderful dinner on our last trip, enjoying splendid food in a splendid place.

- **OPEN:** 5.30pm-10pm Wed-Mon. Closed Nov-Mar
- **PRICE:** Dinner €40
- **CREDIT CARDS:** Visa, Mastercard, Laser

- **NOTES:**

Limited wheelchair access

- **DIRECTIONS:**

Up the hill on Main Street, which connects to Green Street, and The Mall.

10 GREAT

VERNACULAR RESTAURANTS

1
AN CRUIBIN
COUNTY CORK

2
AROMA
COUNTY DONEGAL

3
THE BALLYMORE INN
COUNTY KILDARE

4
KAPPA-YA
COUNTY GALWAY

5
KNOCKRANNY HOUSE
COUNTY MAYO

6
THE OARSMAN
COUNTY LEITRIM

7
THE POACHER'S INN
COUNTY CORK

8
RASAM
COUNTY DUBLIN

9
SAGE
COUNTY MAYO

10
VIEWMOUNT HOUSE
COUNTY LONGFORD

MULCAHY'S

Bruce Mulcahy
36 Henry Street
Kenmare
County Kerry
+353 (0) 64-664 2383

Bruce Mulcahy's restaurant stays on top of its game, year in, year out, a beacon of consistent, creative excellence.

"Six of us had dinner in Bruce's last night", our friend Hannah told us. "Every single dish was perfection. Every single one!" Here's what our friend Billy had to say about Bruce's cooking: "Dined recently in Bruce Mulcahy's. It is all you say and it is more: he deserves every accolade. Bruce is uncompromising when it comes to quality and presentation, and the food is served to the highest standards."
So, how come Bruce Mulcahy isn't a superstar chef, always on the telly and in all the magazines? That's just not the way he works. He doesn't even have a fax machine, far less a website or an internet connection. Self-promotion? No sir. Ego? No sir. What Bruce does is this: he cooks in his restaurant, and every element of his being is devoted to creating the best food he can: scallops with tempura of cauliflower; black sole with tomato and brown butter sauce; crispy duck confit with shredded duck leg salad; crab crème brulée. Perfect service brings all this good stuff together, in a restaurant that is hopelessly dedicated to the art of cooking.

● **OPEN:** 6pm-10pm Mon-Sun (closed Tue & Wed off-season)
● **PRICE:** Dinner from €35
● **CREDIT CARDS:** All major cards accepted.

● **NOTES:**
Wheelchair access. Early bird menu served 6pm-7pm, high season only, €30

● **DIRECTIONS:**
On the right-hand side as you travel down the one-way street, coming from Glengarriff.

OUT OF THE BLUE

Tim Mason
Waterside, Dingle
County Kerry
+353 (0) 66-915 0811
www.outoftheblue.ie
outoftheblue@ireland.com

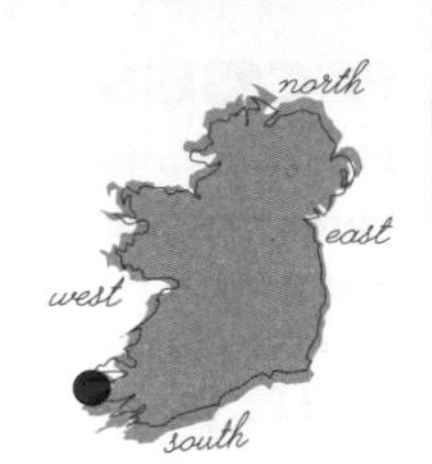

OOTB is one of the Irish restaurant archetypes, a place you dream of finding, the right space in exactly the right place.

The McKenna family are having an Easter lunch in Tim Mason's vital Dingle seafood restaurant, and after a glass or two of wine, and some stunning fish and shellfish, you almost feel like singing "Easter in Dingle/ this is a feeling/no one can ever/ reprise", to the tune of "April in Paris". Ah, Easter in Dingle, what have you done to my heart? Or, more especially, what has Out Of The Blue done to my sensibilities?! The answer to that is, in fact, quite simple. OOTB is an archetypal restaurant, the dream place you are hoping for as you drive towards Dingle that turns out to be real, all too real. It's shacky, simple and super, and the fish cookery is as fine as fish cookery can be - the signature pollock in a potato crust with chive cream; john dory with rosemary; sea bass with tapenade and lemon butter; poached lobster. Combine this with one of the best wine lists in the country, and you have a mighty, magical cocktail of delight. And don't worry: John McKenna didn't burst into song, so no family members or OOTB customers were injured in making this review.

● **OPEN:** 5.30pm-10pm Mon-Sun, closed Wed off season, Lunch 1pm-3.30pm. Closed Nov-Feb
● **PRICE:** Lunch €20-€25, Dinner €45-€50
● **CREDIT CARDS:** Visa, Mastercard, Laser

● **NOTES:**
Wheelchair access to front table in shop. Restaurant closes if they run out of fish. Special "fish deal" menu, first hour of service, €26.50-€32.50

● **DIRECTIONS:**
Directly opposite the main pier in Dingle.

PACKIE'S

Martin Hallissey
Henry Street
Kenmare
County Kerry
+353 (0) 64-664 1508

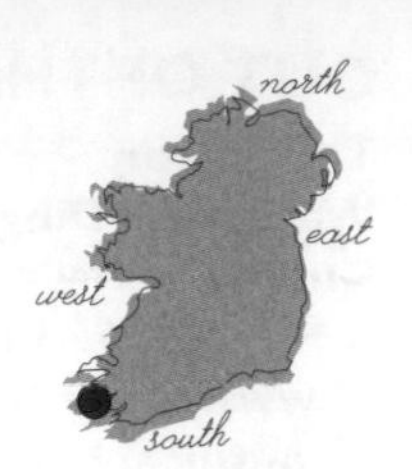

The Packie's manifesto is one of the simplest and most profound: lovely food, lovely room, lovely staff.

Everything in Packie's is understated. Martin Hallissey's brilliance as a chef is to confect his culinary spell from the simplest of ingredients. Other chefs use up-front flavours and cheffy techniques to impress you. But Mr Hallissey just cooks the ingredients as he finds them, and presents them as simply as possible, and the result is spellbinding. His cooking puts us in mind of cucina casalinga – Italian home cooking – in its respect for simplicity and freshness, its understanding of the culture that lies behind a dish, as well as its culinary capability, the need for a dish to be its best, and to be what it is. And from this culture Mr Hallissey brings forth a profound goodness: not to put too fine a point on it, but eating in Packie's is a balm for the soul, and a blessing for the appetite. There is a nurturing quality to the food that few male chefs ever achieve, and the total Packie's experience is not just the food, in particular their seafood cookery, but also the service, which is amongst the very best you will find in Ireland, and also the calm room, which is sublime, simple, just right.

● **OPEN:** 6pm-10pm Mon-Sat. Weekends only off season. Closed mid-Jan to mid-Feb
● **PRICE:** Dinner €30-€45
● **CREDIT CARDS:** Visa, Mastercard, Laser

● **NOTES:**
Wheelchair access, but no disabled toilet.

● **DIRECTIONS:**
In the centre of Kenmare.

THE BALLYMORE INN

Georgina & Barry O'Sullivan
Ballymore Eustace
County Kildare
+353 (0) 45-864 585
www.ballymoreinn.com
theballymoreinn@eircom.net

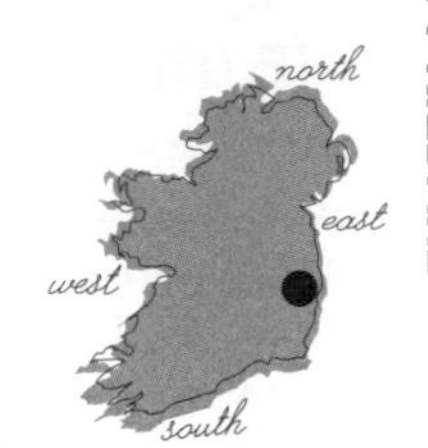

Ten years in the *Bridgestone Guides* for Barry and Georgina O'Sullivan's restaurant, one of the smartest places in Ireland.

It seems astonishing to think that it is now 15 years since Barry and Georgina O'Sullivan opened the doors of the Ballymore Inn, and it's been a decade since the food in the restaurant made its debut in these books, which happened back in 2000. It's been 15 happy years, and a decade of culinary brilliance, in one of the smartest restaurants in Ireland. You can see that smartness at work in the way in which the O'Sullivans frame their food offer, for you can get everything in the BI from a ham and cheese toastie with a bowl of soup for less than a tenner, or you can push out the boat at dinner and enjoy crispy squid with tomato and chilli oil, then West Cork dry-aged sirloin with café de Paris butter, and finish with mature Coolea and Cashel Blue farmhouse cheeses with home-made oat biscuits and quince jelly. Whatever you choose will be true-tasting, it will be of meticulous quality, and it will be drop-dead delicious, and the drama and charm of the room and the energy of the punters will enchant you. If you're planning to open a restaurant, this is how you do it.

● **OPEN:** 12.30pm-9pm Mon-Sun
● **PRICE:** Lunch €20, Dinner €28-€34.50
● **CREDIT CARDS:** Visa, Mastercard, Laser, Amex

● **NOTES:**
Wheelchair access.

● **DIRECTIONS:**
In the centre of Ballymore Eustace, on the right-hand side of the road when coming from Blessington.
GPS 53.1325 -6.610278

THE BROWN BEAR

Fred Cordonnier & Eugene Brennan
Two Mile House
Naas, County Kildare
+353 (0) 45-883 561
www.thebrownbear.ie
jean@thebrownbear.ie

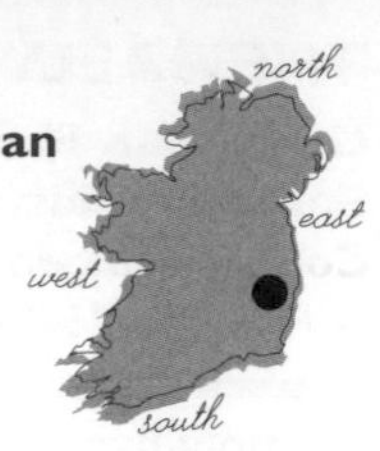

Fred Cordonnier is really putting out the good stuff in The Brown Bear, in Kildare's Two Mile House.

Fred Cordonnier first featured in the *Bridgestone Guides* when he headed up the kitchen at Dublin's Clarence Hotel, and where he quickly distinguished himself as a man with a mature, complete style of cooking. Back in our 2007 Guide, Leslie Williams reckoned Fred was cooking the best lunch in Dublin. Today, M. Cordonnier can till draw the superlatives from discerning food lovers: our friend Eugene wrote to us recently to say that "Fred's cooking was just sublime: every mouthful was a memory, and I would have licked the plate, except I know that if I did, my wife would have broken it over my head". Well, the way Fred is going out here in Two Mile House, a lot of plates are going to be licked, and a lot of plates are going to be broken, for this food is seriously smart, and prices are quite amazing: veal sweetbreads with hand-rolled pasta; breaded crubeen with pickled ox tongue and black pudding soup; wild sea bass with lobster minestrone and anchovy fritter; Rum Baba like they do in Paris. Inspired food, terrific value, a key new address.

● **OPEN:** 6pm-9pm Tue-Fri, 12.30pm-2.30pm, 6pm-9pm Sat, 12.30pm-4pm Sun
● **PRICE:** Dinner €40, Lunch €20
● **CREDIT CARDS:** Visa, Mastercard, Laser

● **NOTES:**
Wheelchair access. Bar open daily from 12.30pm.

● **DIRECTIONS:**
From Naas proceed out the Kilcullen road. Turn right for Two Mile House, go through village, past church and Brown Bear is on the right-hand side.

BASSETT'S AT WOODSTOCK

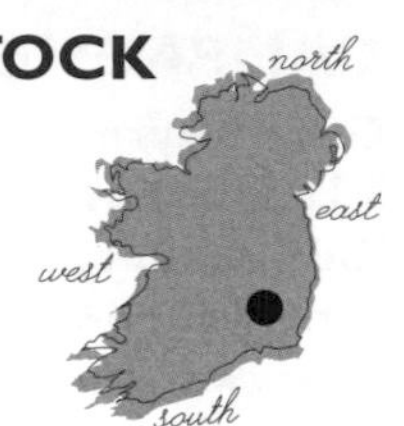

Mijke Jansen & John Bassett
Woodstock Gardens, Inistioge
County Kilkenny
+353 (0) 56-775 8820
www.bassetts.ie
info@bassetts.ie

One of those sport-of-nature restaurants, Bassett's is a gem: unorthodox, inspiring, a place for the true Kilkenny cooking.

Mijke and John's Bassett's place has a charm and a signature that is all its own, the sort of country restaurant that enriches the culture of any county, and of any country. If you found it in the foothills of Piedmont you would reckon it is just so, but in the river valleys of Kilkenny it is equally just so: a little sport of nature, a place unto itself, a place where they do things their own way. It enjoys the most wonderful, romantic location, in the Woodstock demesne, and the beauty of the room is matched by the beauty of Mijke's cooking: cream of garlic soup with aged Parma ham and a slick of balsamic; pan-fried foie gras with onion, vanilla and cumin relish; veal with tuna cream; monkfish with risotto and beetroot purée, all beautifully thought-out and executed. Grilled Wexford lobster is served so simply, with its own bisque and some fresh peas, that it quite takes your breath away, just the sort of grown up cooking that you expect in Bassett's, fusing culinary intelligence with a singular style. Don't miss, in particular, the Saddle Hill lamb. John runs the room with aplomb.

● **OPEN:** noon-4pm, 7.30pm-9.30pm Wed-Sat, 1pm-5pm Sun
● **PRICE:** Lunch €20, Dinner à la carte, €45, sampling menu served Sat, €9.50 per dish, nine dishes
● **CREDIT CARDS:** Visa, Mastercard

● **NOTES:**
Wheelchair access. Dinner: À la carte Wed-Thur, Sampling Sat.

● **DIRECTIONS:**
Follow signs for Woodstock Estate.

CAMPAGNE

Garret Byrne & Brid Hannon
5 The Arches, Gashouse Lane
Kilkenny, County Kilkenny
+353 (0) 56-777 2858
www.campagne.ie
info@campagne.ie

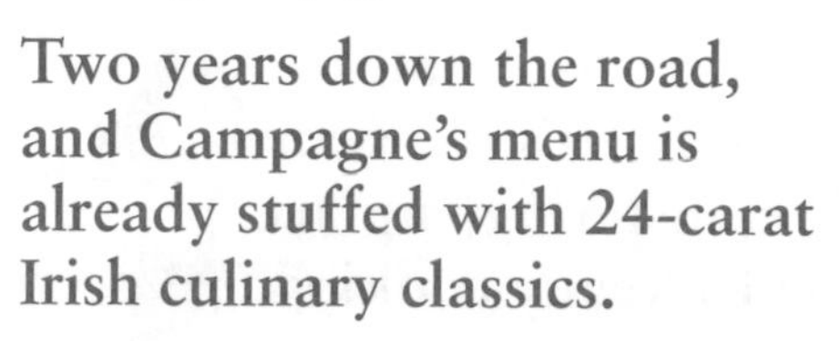

Two years down the road, and Campagne's menu is already stuffed with 24-carat Irish culinary classics.

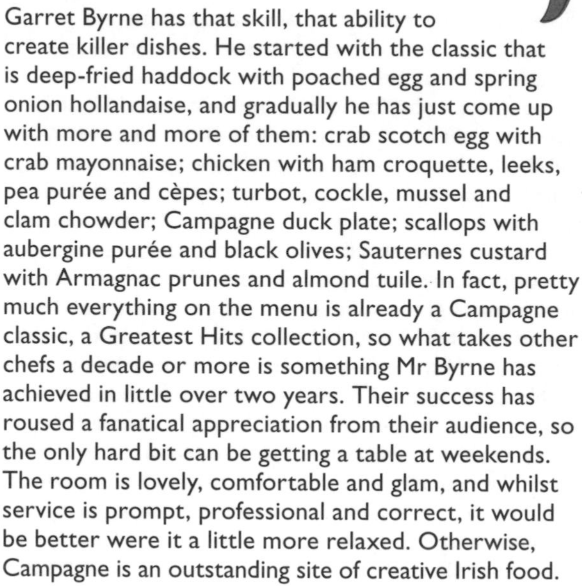

Garret Byrne has that skill, that ability to create killer dishes. He started with the classic that is deep-fried haddock with poached egg and spring onion hollandaise, and gradually he has just come up with more and more of them: crab scotch egg with crab mayonnaise; chicken with ham croquette, leeks, pea purée and cèpes; turbot, cockle, mussel and clam chowder; Campagne duck plate; scallops with aubergine purée and black olives; Sauternes custard with Armagnac prunes and almond tuile. In fact, pretty much everything on the menu is already a Campagne classic, a Greatest Hits collection, so what takes other chefs a decade or more is something Mr Byrne has achieved in little over two years. Their success has roused a fanatical appreciation from their audience, so the only hard bit can be getting a table at weekends. The room is lovely, comfortable and glam, and whilst service is prompt, professional and correct, it would be better were it a little more relaxed. Otherwise, Campagne is an outstanding site of creative Irish food.

- **OPEN:** 12.30pm-2.30pm Fri-Sat, 12.30pm-3.30pm Sun, 6pm-10pm Tue-Sat.
- **PRICE:** Dinner €50, Lunch €24-€28
- **CREDIT CARDS:** All major cards accepted.

- **NOTES:** Full disabled access. Early Bird dinner, €24-€29

- **DIRECTIONS:**

Beside the McDonagh shopping centre on the north side of river. GPS 52.655875 -7.246422

ZUNI

Paul & Paula Byrne
26 Patrick Street
Kilkenny, County Kilkenny
+353 (0) 56-772 3999
www.zuni.ie
info@zuni.ie

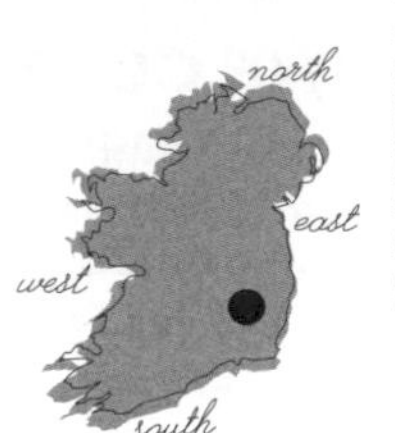

Maria Raftery's cooking has gone up not just one, but several, notches over the last year, and the Zuni kitchen is enjoying a terrific creative spell.

Maria Raftery has really upped her game in Zuni. She has been studying hard in Waterford Institute, bringing new ideas and new techniques back to base in Kilkenny. The impact strikes you immediately: she has gained in confidence through her studies, and the food has more verve and nerve: the walnut dressing on a slice of Helen Finnegan's Knockdrinna goat's cheese is judged pitch perfect; crab in ketaffi pastry with pickled ginger is alive and alert and sets the taste buds on fire, and doesn't everything look so pretty, so poised! Ms Raftery has simplified her main courses to a point of perfection, and the judgement evident in very plate is a delight. The carrot and star anise purée with Skeghanore duck breast is a match made in heaven, and once again her touch with the Asian notes of seared tuna with sesame, bok choi and coriander is right on the money. The great artisan foods of the county are showcased on the menu, and the summertime dinner that John and Connie McKenna enjoyed in this fab room showed that Zuni is experiencing a terrific rebirth.

- **OPEN:** 8am-5pm, tapas from 6pm, Restaurant open 12.30pm-2.30pm, 6pm-9.30pm Mon-Sun
- **PRICE:** Dinner €40-€45, Lunch €26
- **CREDIT CARDS:** All major cards accepted.

- **NOTES:**

Wheelchair access.
Early Bird dinner, Sun-Fri, €23.50-€28.50

- **DIRECTIONS:**

110 metres up Patrick Street from the main traffic junction on the road up to the Castle.

THE COTTAGE RESTAURANT

Sham Hanifa
Jamestown, Carrick-on-Shannon
County Leitrim
+353 (0)71-962 5933
www.cottagerestaurant.ie
info@cottagerestaurant.ie

Sham Hanifa's lovely restaurant is back on track after the floods of the winter, so don't miss this exciting, personal and very different cooking.

Sham Hanifa has a vivid mix of influences in his family, with Thai, Chinese, Malaysian, Indian and Pakistani forebears, and he grew up learning to cook from this huge range of influences. Coming to Ireland in 2000 he started as a commis chef, having worked part-time in restaurants since he was just 13. He worked his way up the ladder, opening The Cottage in Jamestown in 2008, but suffered severe flooding in the torrid winter of 2009. The happy news for Leitrim is that The Cottage is renovated and extended and back in business, and so Mr Hanifa's excellent cooking, in this pretty room, is back on the boil. He is a very fine cook, and he puts in every effort, so elements of a meal frequently taken for granted elsewhere – vegetable cookery, for instance – are top notch here. The food is simple but beautifully executed – sea scallops with crushed black pudding; baked salmon with orange and paprika and a spaghetti of vegetables; sirloin with oxtail potato cake; basil shortbread with summer berry mess. Beautiful food, cooked with imagination and care, and great value.

- **OPEN:** 6pm-10pm Wed-Sun, noon-4pm Sun
- **PRICE:** Dinner €45, Lunch €25
- **CREDIT CARDS:** All major cards accepted.

- **NOTES:**

Wheelchair access.
Early Bird dinner, 5.30pm-7pm €25

- **DIRECTIONS:**

Overlooking Jamestown weir in the village of Jamestown, which is 5km south east of Carrick-on-Shannon.

THE OARSMAN

Ronan & Conor Maher
Bridge Street, Carrick-on-Shannon
County Leitrim
+353 (0) 71-962 1733
www.theoarsman.com
info@theoarsman.com

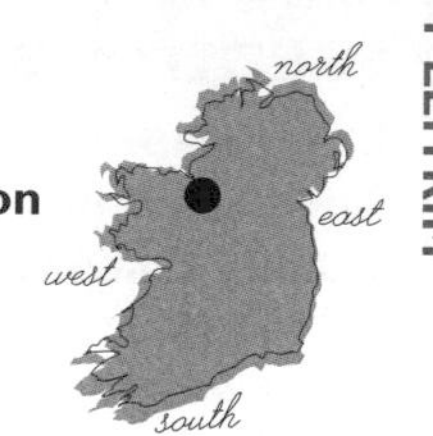

The Maher brothers know how to make the magic in The Oarsman, one of the most atmospheric bars and restaurants in all of Ireland.

One of those moments: you arrive in The Oarsman in the early afternoon on a warm July day. You sit at the bar and order a glass of Galway Hooker whilst you read the menu. You want to eat everything on the menu – the chowder; the chicken salad with soy and ginger; the open prawn sandwich with celeri remoulade, the lot. The beer is a cool oasis of perfection, and so is everything else here: the mood; the lighting; the service; the chatter, the chill. It strikes you that Ronan and Conor Maher simply understand the language of food, the lingua franca of hospitality, the savoir faire of service, and they have communicated their skills to every member of staff. The lunch is perfect in every detail but, more than that, the moment is perfect in every detail, and you don't want to be anywhere other than here, in this darling pub and restaurant. Moments like that don't happen very often, and there aren't that many places that can provoke them. But the Maher boys know how to do it. Boy, do they know how!

- **OPEN:** Bar food noon-9pm Tue-Sat (lunch noon-3pm, afternoon menu 3pm-5pm, dinner 5pm-8.30pm)
- **PRICE:** Lunch €17-€20, Dinner €35-€45
- **CREDIT CARDS:** Visa, Mastercard, Laser

● NOTES:
No children in the bar after 9pm (10pm in summer). Wheelchair access in garden room, no disabled toilet.

● DIRECTIONS:
100m from the Bridge in Carrick centre.

FREDDY'S BISTRO

Liz Phelan
Theatre Lane, Lwr Glentworth St
Limerick, County Limerick
+353 (0) 61-418749
www.freddysbistro.com
info@freddysbristro.com

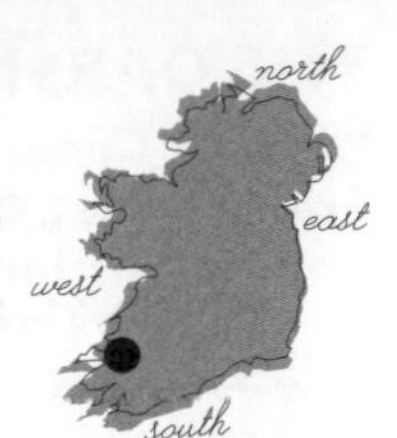

Freddy's has been a fixture of the Limerick scene for some years, but there is always a vivid, youthful, appealing energy in Liz Phelan's bistro.

"This place is gold," said Valerie O'Connor after her last visit to Liz Phelan's bistro on Glentworth Street, a bare-stone, barn-style house with two storeys packed with happy food lovers. And Val isn't alone: "The best meal we had in Ireland" wrote two visting Americans – Jerry and Barbara – after they got back home, in a mail to Bridgestone Central, as unequivocal a thumbs-up! as you can get. So, Ms Phelan is onto something good, based mainly on a concise array of classic dishes from which she extracts the maximum of tactile potential and tactile pleasure: duck pâté is smooth, musky and earthy; mussels in white wine are juicy, plump and peachy sweet. Sea bass in lime leaves will send you to Vietnam on a cloud, whilst rack of lamb with roasted pumpkin is pure comfort cooking. Desserts are rustic and robust – baked orange cheesecake; sticky toffee pudding with butterscotch sauce – pricing is good and service does just what it needs to do, with Liz herself quietly present in an atmospheric room that is powered by the energy of a fired-up kitchen, and happy punters.

- **OPEN:** 5.30pm-late Tue-Sat
- **PRICE:** Dinner €35-€45
- **CREDIT CARDS:** Visa, Mastercard, Laser

● NOTES:
Wheelchair access. Early bird menu €19.95-€24.95

● DIRECTIONS:
Theatre Lane runs between O'Connell Street and Henry Street, near the river in the city centre.

NUMBER ONE PERY SQUARE

Patricia Roberts
1 Pery Sq, The Georgian Quarter
Limerick City, County Limerick
+353 (0) 61-402402
www.oneperysquare.com
info@oneperysquare.com

Chef Alan Burns complements the style of One Pery Square with some glorious modern Irish cooking.

"This is the best of food", says Valerie O'Connor of Alan Burns' cooking in No 1 Pery Square. "It's exciting, fresh, fun and worth talking about". Okay, Val: so talk to us about it."Warm salad of wood pigeon with hazelnut purée and poached cherries was my starter, and also the star of the meal, with warm, musky pigeon nuzzled by a smooth nut purée and a punchy, boozy cherry. Lamb's tongue and beetroot salad was a triumph, the tongue soft and tender, and licked by sweet beets. Main courses were turbot with haricot beans and baby artichokes, and the fish was perfect. Pan-fried cod on buttery clam chowder was a sexy and delicious plate of food, with perfectly cooked, flaky cod resting on oozy, juicy prawns and tiny veggies. Puddings were crème brûlée with a strawberry and lemon balm salad, a perfectly cooked classic, and an incredible sticky toffee pudding, with roasted banana, ginger ice cream and an unctuous caramel sauce. OMG! What a pudding! Alan Burns has the light touch to bring his ingredients together, and value and service are ace."

- **OPEN:** 6pm-9pm Tue-Sat (till 9.30pm Fri & Sat)
- **PRICE:** Dinner €40
- **CREDIT CARDS:** Visa, Mastercard, Laser, Amex

- **NOTES:**

Wheelchair access. Open for breakfast, and afternoon tea in the drawing room, lunch in the Lounge.

- **DIRECTIONS:**

On the corner of Pery Square and Barrington Street.

THE RIVER BISTRO

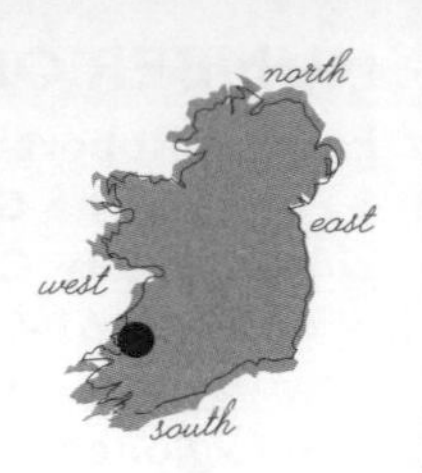

Diarmuid O'Callaghan
4 George's Quay
Limerick, County Limerick

+353 (0) 61-400990

riverbistro@eircom.net
www.theriverbistro.ie

Diarmuid O'Callaghan has graced every place he has cooked in town with great food. His own bistro allows this local hero to shine, with ace food.

Diarmuid O'Callaghan's first chef-patron venture has proven to be a huge success story for this talented cook, a man who first made waves many years ago when he cooked in the great Green Onion Café, when that restaurant was the brightest light in Limerick. Today, his aim in his own place is just as true as back then, and his food continues to enjoy the punchy vivacity of his youth, tempered somewhat by the refinements of experience. He doesn't believe in reinventing the wheel, or fixing something that ain't broke, so there are classics like rack of lamb with crispy rösti, or earthy pork belly with black pudding, or monkfish with pea bombs, or lush desserts like autumn berry crumble. But what makes these classics different is the sensual textures he brings to his food, and the direct, simple salute of the flavours – nothing gets in the way of making the dish pleasurable. The cooking is generous in every way – sensuous, earthy, real and satisfying – and it suits the room, with its winning lack of pretension. So, comfort all the way, then, and no surprise the River Bistro is such a star.

- **OPEN:** 6pm-10pm Tue-Sat
- **PRICE:** Dinner €35 Tue-Fri, €40 Sat
- **CREDIT CARDS:** All major cards accepted

- **NOTES:**

Limited wheelchair access.

- **DIRECTIONS:**

In the centre of Limerick, near the Courthouse, the Locke Bar and Barrington's Hospital.

THE WILD GEESE

David Foley & Julie Randles
Rose Cottage, Main Street
Adare, County Limerick
+353 (0) 61-396451
www.thewild-geese.com
wildgeese@indigo.ie

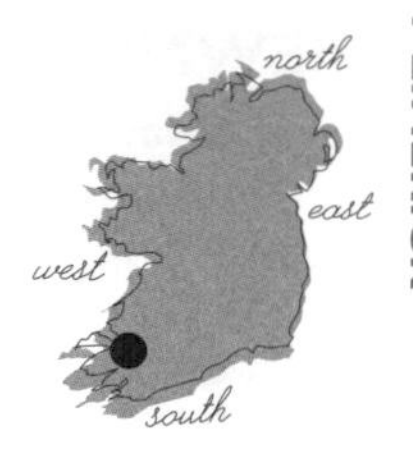

It's been a long time since we first ate David Foley's food, and we have never known him to produce an indifferent dish.

David and Julie have been at the helm of the beautiful Wild Geese restaurant for a decade, and have done nothing more during that time other than get better, and better, and better. The secret of their success is simple: the alliance of their respective talents is an extraordinary synthesis: she is magisterial at front-of-house, he is dynamic and creative in the kitchen, and we mean it when we say there isn't a better him 'n' her team in the country. They're the tops, they're the Mona Lisa. Put this lovely cooking and sublime service together with the most romantic dining space – this may actually be the MOST romantic room in the country – and you have nothing less than magic. The food is simply adorable, well-crafted and understood, and ever since we first ate Mr Foley's food in a Dublin hotel – back in the day, as they say – we have never known him to produce a bad dish. So, Curraghchase sausage with champ and smoked bacon jus, or perhaps cod and crabmeat with a mussel and clam risotto, or Adare spring lamb with rosemary. Perfect in every detail.

- **OPEN:** 6.30pm-10pm Tue-Sat, 12.30pm-3pm Sun.
- **PRICE:** Dinner €35-€48
- **CREDIT CARDS:** Visa, Mastercard, Laser, Amex

NOTES:
Wheelchair access but no disabled toilet. Early bird Tue-Fri, 6.30pm-7.30pm (till 7pm on Sat), €29-€35

DIRECTIONS:
On the Main Street of Adare village, near the gates of Adare Manor and just opposite the Dunraven Arms.

VIEWMOUNT HOUSE

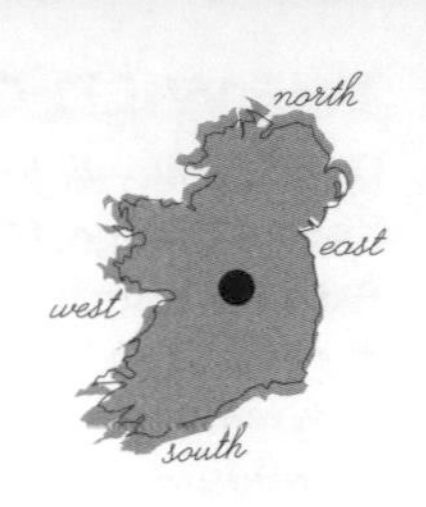

Beryl & James Kearney
Dublin Road, Longford
County Longford
+353 (0) 43-334 1919
www.viewmounthouse.com
info@viewmounthouse.com

Boy, but Viewmount House is the happening place in Longford, a room with mighty energy, and mighty food.

So, there are all the McKennas in VM restaurant, laughing their socks off about the news story about the guys who p-p-picked up a penguin from Dublin Zoo, and it seems that everyone else in the room is in on the joke, because the energy here on a weekend night is only seismic. VM is buzzing, the toast of the town thanks to Gary O'Hanlon's brilliant cooking, and some superb service under the eye of Beryl Kearney. And as the evening wears on, the energy only gets better, fuelled by some inspired cooking. Mr O'Hanlon likes complex food that eats simple: his vegetarian degustation starter, for instance, has Glebe Brethan cheese, tomato confit, baby beets, pears, candied walnuts, enoki, white truffle honey swede, St Tola goats' cheese and Donegal rapeseed oil. It isn't a dish: it's a tapestry, a mosaic of flavours and textures, and it is stunning. But so is everything: wonton of slow-cooked Jacob's Ladder; Kettyle chicken with mushroom froth; pan-seared john dory with scallion and pea risotto, and pastry chef Sammie Straume's desserts are amazing to behold. Hot.

- **OPEN:** 6.30pm-9.30pm Wed-Sat, 1pm-4.30pm Sun
- **PRICE:** Lunch €29, Dinner €55
- **CREDIT CARDS:** Visa, Mastercard, Laser, Amex

- **NOTES:**

Wheelchair access. Wed & Thu menu, €40.

- **DIRECTIONS:**

From the M4, at the first roundabout entering Longford, take the first exit for town centre. You will see their sign on the left-hand side. GPS 53.72246 -7.77105

ROSSO

Louisa Gilhooly
5 Roden Place, Dundalk
County Louth
+353 (0) 42-935 6502
www.rossorestaurant.com
enquiries@rossorestaurant.com

Louisa Gilhooly's Rosso, with chef Danielle Barry in the kitchen, is proving that it has just the right formula for a cautious town like Dundalk.

Louisa Gilhooly manages the room, head chef Danielle Barry rattles the pans, and Rosso has been the star destination in Dundalk ever since they opened their doors. Ms Barry's food is smart, feminine and wise, and it showcases a kitchen team that is ambitious and on top of their game. We love the games they play with their ingredients, the fun they have resurrecting cordon bleu standards into contemporary classics, like caramelised onion tart with blue cheese and candied walnut salad, or chicken supreme with leeks, onion gnocchi, pancetta and peas, or lamb niçoise with dauphinoise potatoes. It's clever food, but it's never, ever clever-clever, for Ms Barry is too hip to do that, and yet if you weren't of a mind to think too much about what you are eating, you would simply say that the food is delicious, for the artfulness never gets in the way. Prices are good for such fine ingredients and such careful cooking, and vegetarians should note that there is a proper menu of vegetarian choices. The café upstairs has a very good breakfast and lunch offering.

● **OPEN:** 12.30pm-2.30pm, 6pm-9.30pm Tue-Fri, 6pm-10pm Sat, 12.30pm-4.30pm Sun
● **PRICE:** Lunch €12.50, Dinner €40
● **CREDIT CARDS:** Visa, Mastercard, Laser

● **NOTES:**
No wheelchair access. Pre-theatre dinners 6pm-7pm, Tue-Fri, €25.50

● **DIRECTIONS:**
Directly opposite St Patrick's Cathedral.

KNOCKRANNY HOUSE

Adrian & Ger Noonan
Westport
County Mayo
+353 (0) 98-28600
www.khh.ie
info@khh.ie

Seamus Commons' cooking in La Fougere is the brightest star in the West, a cataclysmic, modern Irish cuisine.

To write about Seamus Commons' cooking, you have to revert either to extreme simplicity – "This is one chef who sure can cook", was how the food writer Aoife Carrigy appositely summed him up – or else you have to go for the "War and Peace" approach: give me several hundred pages and I will describe the outrageous event that is the tasting menu in the La Fougere restaurant in the Knockranny House Hotel. But somewhere in between lies the key to this man's cooking, and we think his signature is simply that he works harder than anyone else. Even the simplest plate – wild Atlantic halibut seared, house smoked salmon panna cotta, fennel & lime, cauliflower, curried velouté – is an elaborate quilt of tastes, textures and temperatures that hide the enormous effort – that smoked salmon is smoked in-house, for example. His other secret is that there is never a detail out of place: everything synthesises with everything else, making for cooking that is amongst the most exciting, creative and original in Ireland. This is one chef who sure can cook!

- **OPEN:** 6.30pm-9.30pm Mon-Sat, 7pm-9.30pm Sun
- **PRICE:** Dinner €54
- **CREDIT CARDS:** Visa, Mastercard, Amex,

- **NOTES:**

Wheelchair access. Bar food available in Brehon Bar. Bar Lunch Mon-Sat.

- **DIRECTIONS:**

Off the Dublin/Castlebar Road, 10mins from Westport town centre. GPS 53.80306 -9.50806

SAGE

Davide Dannaloia & Sarah Hudson
10 High Street, Westport
County Mayo
+353 (0) 98-56700
www.sagewestport.ie
info@sagewestport.ie

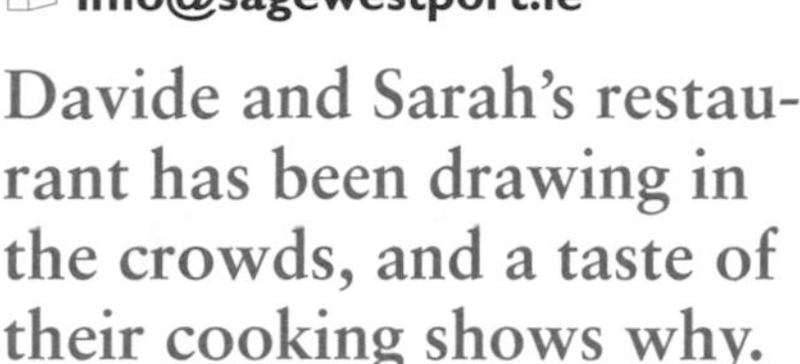

Davide and Sarah's restaurant has been drawing in the crowds, and a taste of their cooking shows why.

Davide Dannaloia has always been very clear about what he wants to achieve with his food in Sage, the little restaurant he runs with his partner, Sarah Hudson. He has the nerve, for instance, to dare to be simple, to recognise what he is good at and to base his offer on that template of dishes which shows his skills and his temperament at their best – his homemade ravioli with ricotta and spinach; a plate of roasted, marinated vegetables; his gnocchi with Gorgonzola sauce and walnuts; his signature slow-roast pork belly with a casserole of beans, chorizo and sweet peppers. The result is some of the most authentic, most rustic cooking you will find in Ireland, food with an Italian accent but a west coast voice. Sticking to his vision of what he wants to achieve meant some quiet nights in the early days, but summer 2010 proved that word about this food had spread, for Davide and Sarah were rushed off their feet and the little room was jammers. So, open that Pinot Grigio, bring me the lobster with linguini, and sure we may as well have that fine chocolate fondue for pudding.

- **OPEN:** 5.30pm-10pm Tue-Sun
- **PRICE:** Dinner €30
- **CREDIT CARDS:** Visa, Mastercard, Laser

NOTES:
Wheelchair access
Early bird menu, 5.30pm-7pm, €18

DIRECTIONS:
Westport town centre.

10 PLACES

FOR VEGETARIANS

1. ARD BIA
COUNTY GALWAY

2. BAR NO 8
COUNTY GALWAY

3. THE BAY TREE
COUNTY DOWN

4. AN CRUIBIN
COUNTY CORK

5. GINGER
COUNTY ANTRIM

6. GRANGECON CAFÉ
COUNTY WICKLOW

7. MACNEAN RESTAURANT
COUNTY CAVAN

8. 101 TALBOT
COUNTY DUBLIN

9. RASAM
COUNTY DUBLIN

10. THE WINDING STAIR
COUNTY DUBLIN

THE RESTAURANT AT NUREMORE

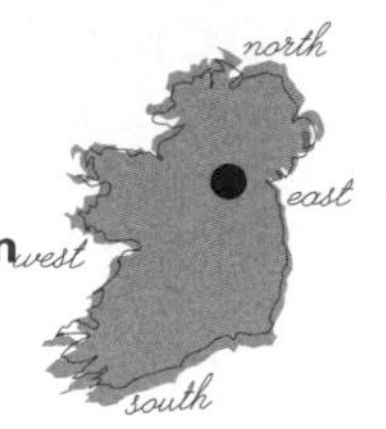

Julie Gilhooly, Nuremore Hotel
Carrickmacross, County Monaghan
+353 (0) 42-966 1438
www.nuremore.com
info@nuremore.com

The Nuremore Hotel is comfortable, whilst Ray McArdle's cooking is quite simply a cutting-edge contemporary concoction: it's right out there.

It was Marco Pierre White who made young Ray McArdle want to be a chef. Today, more than twenty years later, and Mr McArdle is still pushing the envelope of cookery's possibilities and potentials. His hunger to explore gives his cooking great motivation and youthfulness: here is a chef who never rests on his laurels, a man for whom every new cheffy adventure that happens offers a chance to experiment, a challenge to explore. But Mr McArdle isn't, like many chefs, a mere copyist. He will take new ideas, but will then meld them to his own métier, so the fashions for foams, or for Asian spices, or for sweet and savoury ingredients to be allied together, will be utilised here in the Nuremore, but what emerges is always a Ray McArdle dish: carpaccio and char-grilled tuna with fennel and cucumber dressing; Kettyle fillet steak with deconstructed chasseur sauce (literary post-modernism in Kavanagh country!); roast Wexford scallops with cannelloni of crab and courgette and orange foam; iced orange parfait with mulled wine sorbet. Dazzling food.

● **OPEN:** 12.30pm-2.30pm, 6.30pm-9.30pm Mon-Sun (no lunch on Sat, closed 9pm Sun)
● **PRICE:** Lunch €25, Dinner €40-€80
● **CREDIT CARDS:** Visa, Mastercard, Amex

● **NOTES:**
Wheelchair access - ramp from car park, no steps to restaurant.

● **DIRECTIONS:**
1.5km south of Carrickmacross on the principal N2, Dublin-Derry route, signposted at the entrance.

BROCKA ON THE WATER

Anthony & Anne Gernon
Kilgarvan Quay
Ballinderry
County Tipperary
+353 (0) 67-22038

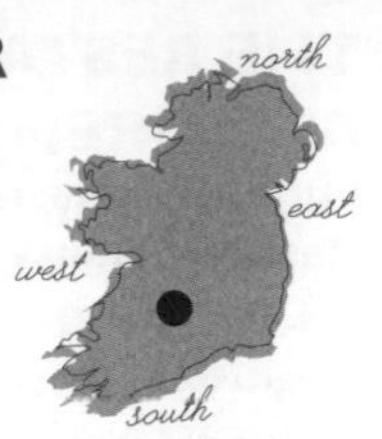

Grannie Nancy has stepped back, whilst granddaughter Judy has stepped forward into the beautiful, unique Brocka.

Anthony, Anne and Judy's Brocka On The Water was one of the four Tipperary restaurants to host the 2010 Tipperary Top Table dinners – the others were Chez Hans, Inch House and The Old Convent. Anne cooked Inch House black pudding with Scullery onion marmalade; deep-fried Cooleeney cheese croquettes with chutney; Michael Seymour's organic lamb with aubergine and Country Choice pesto; Dorothy Harding's chicken with Lakeshore mustard cream, and baked Tipperary garden potatoes from Brocka with garlic butter. Pudding was their classic meringues with Bouleabane ice cream, and stewed berry fruits with shortbread crumble. Wow! Is that a menu of local foods to have you dreaming and drooling, or what! Such simplicity, such wisdom, such modesty, and to be able to enjoy it in this beautiful family home, which also just happens to be a restaurant, is really as good as local food and cooking can be. Nowhere else is quite like Brocka, this enchanting little tabernacle of food, this aesthetic dream, this powerhouse of family food and creativity.

- **OPEN:** 7pm-10pm Mon-Sat. Reservations only.
- **PRICE:** Dinner €55
- **CREDIT CARDS:** No credit cards

- **NOTES:**

Wheelchair access. Booking essential off season.

- **DIRECTIONS:**

On Kilgarvan Quay on the Lough Derg Drive, half way between Nenagh and Portumna. From the N52, turn at Borrisokane for Ballinderry.

CHEZ HANS & CAFÉ HANS

Jason Matthiae,
Stefan & Hansi Matthiae, Moor Lane
Cashel, County Tipperary
● **Chez Hans +353 (0) 62-61177**
● **Café Hans +353 (0) 62-63660**
www.chezhans.net

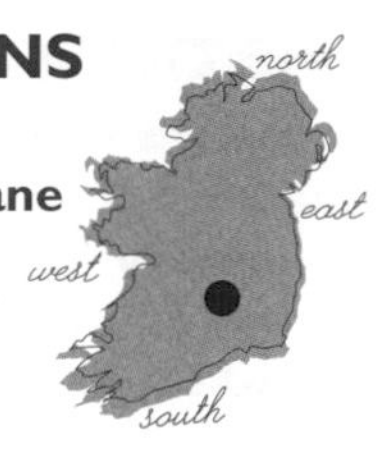

Folks in the know will know that Café Hans and Chez Hans are both producing some of the very best cooking.

"Best? Café Hans in Cashel". That's what Ian and Lorraine from Belfast wrote after a wonderful gastronomic tour of Ireland using the *Bridgestone Guide*. We quote it to show you the level at which Café Hans is operating, for Ian and Lorraine ate at lots of cutting-edge places throughout the country, and yet Hansi and Steffie's daytime café beat all the superstars to take the top spot. Mind you, had they had the chance to try brother Jason's food in Chez Hans, just down the street, we have no doubt that they would have put it right up there with the Café. For Chez Hans is the other side of the coin to the Café – more formal, more elaborate – yet the creative dynamic that unites these brothers is identical in both places. Jason's riffing on modern dishes in Chez Hans is brilliantly orchestrated, never more so than at a recent Tipperary Top Table dinner when the kitchen cooked a magnificent culinary tour through the county's best ingredients, from Munster mushrooms to Pat Whelan's dry-aged beef, a dinner that made you feel you were at the centre of the culinary world.

● **OPEN:** 6pm-10pm Tue-Sat (Chez Hans); noon-5.30pm Tue-Sat (Café Hans)
● **PRICE:** Lunch (Café) €20, Dinner (Chez) €40-€60
● **CREDIT CARDS:** Visa, Mastercard, Laser (Chez Hans). No credit cards accepted in Café Hans.

● **NOTES:**
Wheelchair access. No bookings taken in Café Hans. Early Bird menu 6pm-8pm, €28-€35 in Chez Hans Tue-Thu, 6pm-7pm Fri.

● **DIRECTIONS:**
Just beside the Rock of Cashel.

THE OLD CONVENT

Dermot & Christine Gannon
Clogheen
County Tipperary
+353 (0) 52-7465565
www.theoldconvent.ie
info@theoldconvent.ie

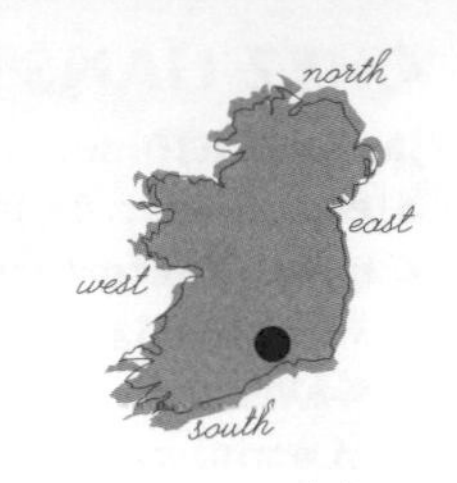

Dermot and Christine's The Old Convent is right up there at the top of the tree for a unique Irish experience.

Dermot Gannon was washing pots for Tim O'Sullivan in Renvyle House in Connemara when he was a kid, and aged 17 he went to work for Paddy Foyle in Rosleague, and later in Destry's in Clifden. It would be hard to get better mentors than these two enlightened, creative professionals, and Mr Gannon was always keen to learn, and always learnt well. In The Old Convent, a delightful, comfortable old pile just on the edge of Clogheen, he has synthesised the influences of his mentors, and arrived at a locally-based cuisine that is amongst the most exciting in Ireland. When Eamon Barrett ate here, he described the tasting menu as "a near-perfect experience", and the eight courses are a giddy waltz through Ireland's best foods, orchestrated by a modern master. As befits a Connemara man, he does bring in some west coast ingredients, with the odd blow-in from nearby Cork, such as Jack McCarthy's beef. But mostly it is local foods ennobled by great skill to give a true sense of modern Irish food at its glorious best. A star pupil.

- **OPEN:** Dinner served at 8pm Thu-Sat & bank holiday Sundays. Closed Christmas-end of Jan
- **PRICE:** 8-course tasting menu, €65
- **CREDIT CARDS:** Visa, Master, Laser

NOTES:

No wheelchair access. Children over 12 years welcome to dining room. Guesthouse over 18s only.

DIRECTIONS:

On the R668 Cahir to Lismore road. A detailed map is available from their website.

L'ATMOSPHERE

Arnaud & Patrice Mary
19 Henrietta Street, Waterford
County Waterford
+353 (0) 51-858426
www.restaurant-latmosphere.com
Latmosphererestaurant@hotmail.com

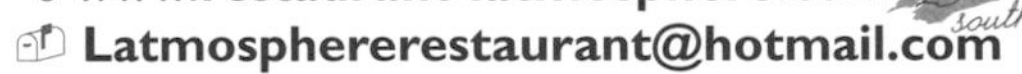

Arnaud Mary understands the economy of the kitchen, and it results in incredible value for money, and in incredible cooking for his customers.

Arnaud Mary is not only a great chef, he's a great restaurateur, fully understanding the commercial reality of keeping your tables full, offering the most lip-smackingly good food, and keeping prices keen. He does this by not buying just fillets and sirloins and prime cuts from his suppliers, as has become the norm with so many chefs. No way: this guy buys the whole beast and uses as near as dammit every single bit. So while you may not know which part of the cow an onglet or a bavette come from, you can trust Arnaud that he knows, and that they will be super flavoursome. "The crux of all this though, the USP if you like, is that although our choices amounted to luxury dining, Arnaud's soul is rooted in value and flavour, in the use of cheaper cuts of meat and braising, so you can still have the early bird for €20, or a great lamb main course for €14.50. The sheer quality of L'Atmosphere is a wonderful shock," says Eamon Barrett "A wonderful shock": what a brilliant way to describe the charm of a great destination, and this inspiring restaurant never puts a foot wrong.

- **OPEN:** 12.30pm-2.30pm, 5.30pm-late Mon-Fri, 5.30pm-late Sat & Sun
- **PRICE:** Lunch €13 main dish, Dinner €20-€35
- **CREDIT CARDS:** Visa, Master, Laser

● NOTES:
Wheelchair access.

● DIRECTIONS:
The narrow Henrietta St. runs off the waterfront close to the Reginald's Tower end of the main quay.

CLIFF HOUSE HOTEL

Adriaan Bartels
Ardmore
County Waterford
+ 353 (24) 87 800
www.thecliffhousehotel.com
info@thecliffhousehotel.com

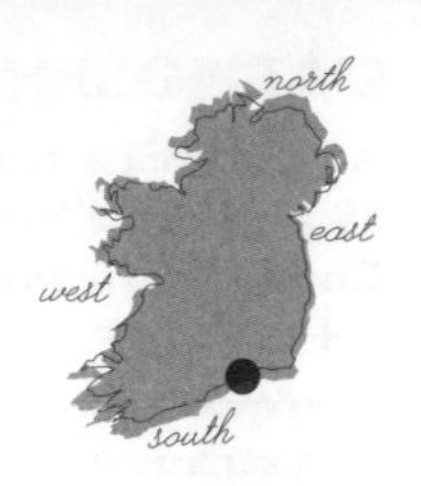

Cliff House is radical, with seriously creative, original cooking from the brilliantly talented Martijn Kajuiter.

The Cliff House Hotel is a pearl – it clings to the cliff in Ardmore in a miraculous feat of engineering, and the interior style is just breathtaking – and inside that pearl is the pearl that is chef Martijn Kajuiter's cuisine. If the design template is bold, the culinary template is bolder still. Here is a man who has subsumed all the current European mannerisms of modern restaurant cooking, and trained them up into a striking cuisine of his own. It's an holistic cuisine, embracing everything edible from shoreline to farm to wild foods to edible flowers, and the precision of the cooking means everything is plosive with flavour and full of surprises, like juniper berry ice cream with pigeon, or chive flowers with marsh samphire, or radish and dried fennel with West Cork scallops, or the daringly barely-sweet desserts. Confident, opinionated, radical – incidentally Mr Kajuiter tweets the same way he cooks – this is food for the senses and for the intellect, good to eat and good to think. The setting is stupendous, of course, and value for money is excellent.

- **OPEN:** 6.30pm-10pm Mon-Sun.
- **PRICE:** Dinner €65-€85
- **CREDIT CARDS:** Visa, Access, Master, Amex, Laser

- **NOTES:** Full wheelchair access. Bar open daily and serves food noon-9pm, booking advisable at weekends.

- **DIRECTIONS:**

From the N25 turn onto the R673 signposted Ardmore. Once in Ardmore take Middle Road to hotel. GPS 51.948614 -7.715078

O'BRIEN CHOP HOUSE

Justin & Jenny Green
Main Street, Lismore
County Waterford
+ 353 (0) 58-53810
www.obrienchophouse.ie
info@obrienchophouse.ie

Justin, Eddie and Richard are really firing on all cylinders in O'Brien Chop House: they're on a roll.

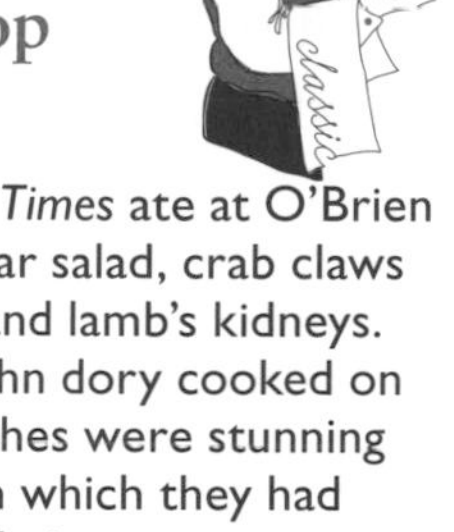

When Nick Lander of the *Financial Times* ate at O'Brien Chop House, he started with Caesar salad, crab claws with wild garlic and lemon butter, and lamb's kidneys. All good, but then came a whole john dory cooked on the bone, and rib of beef. "Both dishes were stunning in their sourcing, the precision with which they had been cooked and the simplicity of their presentation... almost as good were the puddings: lemon tart; rhubarb mess; chocolate mousse cake and brown bread ice cream."

Nick Lander isn't the only one to have been gob-smacked by the food in Justin Green's delightful Chop House. The mighty trio of talents here – Mr Green of Ballyvolane House; chef Eddie Bagulo and manager Richard Reeve – have been doing everything right from the day they opened their doors, and it's not just the day-to-day stuff that knocks your socks off: when Caroline Hennessy came here for their Green Saffron curry and Dungarvan Beer night, she was blown away by the food, the energy and the achievement. Mighty.

- **OPEN:** Open from noon, lunch 12.30pm-3pm, tea 3pm-6pm, dinner 6.30pm-9.30pm Wed-Sat (closed Wed off season)
- **PRICE:** Lunch €22.90-€27.90, Dinner €35
- **CREDIT CARDS:** All major credit cards accepted

- **NOTES:**

Wheelchair access.

- **DIRECTIONS:**

On the main street in Lismore, left as you head up the street from the N72.

RICHMOND HOUSE

Paul & Claire Deevy
Cappoquin
County Waterford
+353 (0) 58-54278
www.richmondhouse.net
info@richmondhouse.net

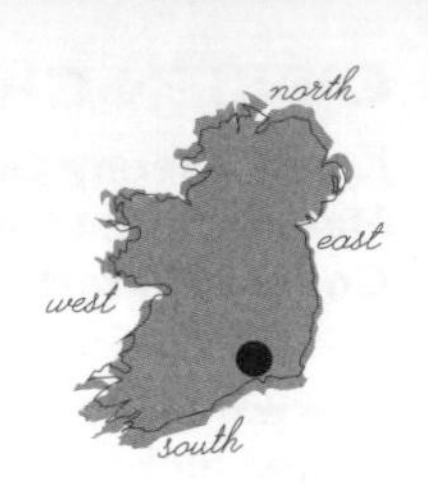

Paul and Claire's understated country house is just what a country house should be: charming, hospitable, happy.

Paul and Claire Deevy's country house and restaurant is one of Ireland's very best. There is a calmness, a generosity, a true understanding of hospitality and an almost anti-commercial ambience in Richmond House that really does make it feel like a visit to a friend, rather than a visit to a commercially-run country house hotel. In tandem with the very personal style of the house, Mr Deevy's cooking is subtle, pure, satisfying, and he has such knowledge of, and respect for, his local foods that every meal we have eaten here over the last fifteen years has been memorable and delicious. He loves the gentleness of flavours such as sweet cicely in a cleansing sorbet, or the clean tang of lovage in a potato soup, or fresh chives in a mayonnaise to pair with a tian of local crabmeat, and then he also cooks the classics as if they were freshly minted, bringing a fresh touch to fillet steak with champ and bearnaise, or fillet of Waterford lamb with rosemary jus. The charm of the house and the delightful, low-key but friendly service, brings even more nobility to this great cooking.

- **OPEN:** 7pm-9pm Tue-Sun (closed Sun off season)
- **PRICE:** Dinner €55
- **CREDIT CARDS:** Visa, Mastercard, Laser

- **NOTES:** Recommended for vegetarians. Wheelchair access to restaurant only. Early Bird 6pm-7pm €28-€33. 9 guest rooms. Sun lunch on bank hols

- **DIRECTIONS:**

Just outside Cappoquin, heading in the direction of Waterford city. GPS 52.139261 -7.846708

THE TANNERY RESTAURANT

Paul & Máire Flynn
10 Quay Street, Dungarvan
County Waterford
+353 (0) 58-45420
www.tannery.ie
tannery@cablesurf.com

Paul Flynn is getting the respect he and his cooking deserve as his school allows him to spread the Tannery's philosophy.

He's too young to be an elder statesman of Irish cooking, is Paul Flynn, but there is no question that he now holds a position at the pinnacle of his peers, or that his efforts as a teacher in the Tannery Cookery School have enabled him to spread his philosophy about good cooking and good food. If you didn't know about the philosophy, you would simply say that The Tannery is a brilliant Irish restaurant. But when you encompass the whole, modest, holistic ambit of Mr Flynn's ideas on food, then you will look at his work in a different light. You will understand how important he is, how singular his cooking is, and how much he has contributed to Irish food over the last dozen or more years. Mind you, when the McKenna children were enjoying dinner in the Tannery during the Dungarvan food festival this year, they were likely only thinking that the roast pumpkin soup was wicked, and so was the crab crème brûlée and the crispy corned beef rolls and the rib-eye with pickled wild mushrooms, and the gratin of blackberries. Fab.

● **OPEN:** 6pm-9.30pm Tue-Sat, lunch served Fri & Sun noon-2.30pm. Open Sun bank hols and August.
● **PRICE:** Lunch €30, Dinner €50
● **CREDIT CARDS:** Visa, Mastercard, Laser, Amex

● **NOTES:** Wheelchair access. Early bird menu Tue-Fri, 6pm-7.15pm, €28.50. The Tannery guesthouse and Cookery School also recommended.

● **DIRECTIONS:**
Situated beside the Old Market House building.
GPS 52.08864 -7.61677

WATERFORD CASTLE

Michael Quinn
Waterford Castle, The Island
Ballinakill, County Waterford
+353 (0) 51-878203
www.waterfordcastle.com
info@waterfordcastle.com

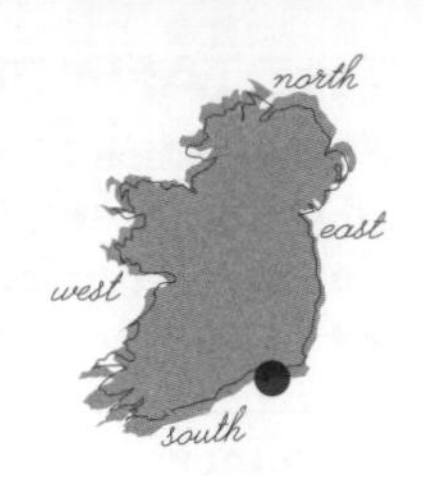

Say it loud: Michael Quinn is one of the greatest Irish cooks, and as time goes by he gets better and better.

Michael Quinn is one of the best cooks in Ireland, and he is also a very nice, quiet, gentlemanly guy, a bloke who pours his heart and his soul into his work. His cooking is simply top-notch, not just a brilliantly realised vision of what sophisticated modern Irish food can be, but also a very personal cuisine that links straight back to his personality, his instinct and his desire to please. And so, he cooks food in the lovely Waterford Castle that is deeply pleasing, deeply enjoyable, from his sweet, rich Dunmore East lobster risotto with tarragon, through Castle smoked duck salad with candied pecans, via fried wild sea bass with samphire, or his classic essays with beef and lamb, where he cooks Comeragh lamb three ways, and adds crisp oxtail and a cep cream to O'Flynn's beef. The sourcing of the ingredients simply couldn't be bettered, service is gracious, and all the details chime together in this grand room, where Mr Quinn proves that his cuisine is an extension of his personality and his philosophy, and that both personality and philosophy are modest and wise.

- **OPEN:** 6.30pm-9pm Mon-Sun
- **PRICE:** Dinner €65
- **CREDIT CARDS:** Visa, Mastercard, Amex

NOTES:
Wheelchair access.

DIRECTIONS:
5km out of Waterford on the Dunmore East Road. They operate their own ferry to the island.

10 GREAT

PLACES FOR SEAFOOD

1

CLIFF HOUSE HOTEL
COUNTY WATERFORD

2

FISHY FISHY CAFÉ
COUNTY CORK

3

GLOBAL VILLAGE
COUNTY KERRY

4

HARRY'S BAR & RESTAURANT
COUNTY DONEGAL

5

MICHIE SUSHI
COUNTY DUBLIN

6

MOURNE SEAFOOD BAR
COUNTY ANTRIM

7

OSCAR'S
COUNTY GALWAY

8

OUT OF THE BLUE
COUNTY KERRY

9

SHU
COUNTY ANTRIM

10

THE TANNERY
COUNTY WATERFORD

LA DOLCE VITA

Roberto & Celine Pons
6-7 Trimmer's Lane
Wexford
County Wexford
+353 (0) 53-917 0806
bigpons@eircom.net

Tiny, dramatic gestures in every dish make Roberto Pons' Italian cooking a thing of joy and delight in the brilliant, busy, bustling La Dolce Vita.

Roberto Pons now cooks at weekend evenings in La Dolce Vita, trying to satisfy the insatiable hunger for his superb cooking amongst the good folk of Wexford. His Italian cooking, like the best Italian cooking, is packed with tiny gestures, tiny dramas, that work to transform simple things into special – but still simple – things: the slow-roasted tomatoes with gazzetta of prawns and cannellini beans that fills out the sweetness of the prawns with the concentrated sweetness of the tomatoes; the perfectly roasted and perfectly oozing roast garlic that acts as taste foil to sweet and delicious lamb chops; the deep, concentrated and utterly perfect red wine sauce that works to flesh out the earthy, feral flavour of wild venison; and when it comes to sweet things, what you will find in La Dolce Vita is as good a tiramisu as is made in the Northern hemisphere. Daytime, the place is a riot of activity as hungry folk wait for happy, sated folk to give up their tables. It's more relaxed in the evenings, but at any time LDV is a restaurant that pulses with the pleasure of great food.

- **OPEN:** 9am-5.30pm Mon-Fri, 9.30am-9.30pm Sat
- **PRICE:** Lunch mains €9-€15
- **CREDIT CARDS:** Visa, Mastercard, Laser

- **NOTES:**

Wheelchair access.

- **DIRECTIONS:**

In the Selskar part of Wexford town.

KELLY'S RESORT HOTEL

Eugene Callaghan
Rosslare
County Wexford
+353 (0) 53-913 2114
www.kellys.ie

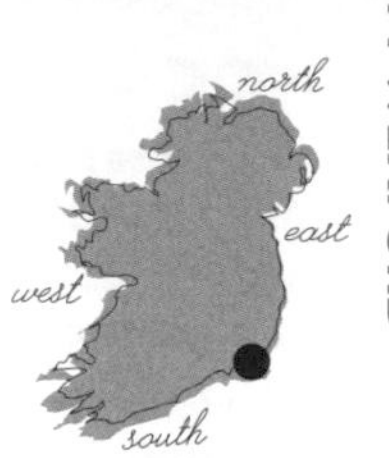

Eugene Callaghan is the best, a chef whose culinary explorations create benchmarks in terms of taste and texture.

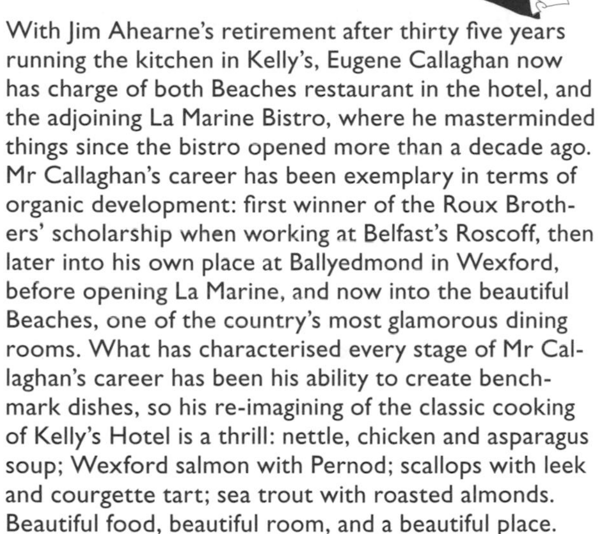

With Jim Ahearne's retirement after thirty five years running the kitchen in Kelly's, Eugene Callaghan now has charge of both Beaches restaurant in the hotel, and the adjoining La Marine Bistro, where he masterminded things since the bistro opened more than a decade ago. Mr Callaghan's career has been exemplary in terms of organic development: first winner of the Roux Brothers' scholarship when working at Belfast's Roscoff, then later into his own place at Ballyedmond in Wexford, before opening La Marine, and now into the beautiful Beaches, one of the country's most glamorous dining rooms. What has characterised every stage of Mr Callaghan's career has been his ability to create benchmark dishes, so his re-imagining of the classic cooking of Kelly's Hotel is a thrill: nettle, chicken and asparagus soup; Wexford salmon with Pernod; scallops with leek and courgette tart; sea trout with roasted almonds. Beautiful food, beautiful room, and a beautiful place.

● **OPEN:** Beaches open for non residents lunch and dinner, La Marine open 12.30pm-2.15pm, 6.30pm-9pm Mon-Sun. Hotel closed early Dec-late Feb

● **PRICE:** La Marine lunch menu from €7-€25, Dinner from €34, Beaches lunch €25-€28 and dinner €45

● **CREDIT CARDS:** Visa, Mastercard, Laser, Amex

● **NOTES:**
Wheelchair access with advance notice. Off season early bird menu, 6.30pm-7.15pm, Sun-Thurs, €23-€28

● **DIRECTIONS:**
Kelly's Hotel is well signposted from in the area. La Marine has a separate entrance.

AVOCA

Simon Pratt ● Avoca Village 0402-35105 ● Mount Usher Gardens, Ashford 0404-40205 ● Kilmacanogue 01-274 6990 ● Powerscourt 01-204 6066 ● Rathcoole 01-257 1800 ● Suffolk St 01-677 4215 ● Letterfrack 095-41058 ● Moll's Gap 064-663 4720 ● 41 Arthur St, Belfast +44 28-90 279 950 www.avoca.ie

north
east
west
south

Avoca is where you see people finding God in the detail, in the smallest gesture. It sure makes you feel good.

It's knowing that God is in the detail that makes Avoca different. The Hegarty brothers' cheddar with a beef burger in Egg, the Rathcoole restaurant. The Gold River Farm organic cauliflower cheese in the Garden Café at Mount Usher. The Avoca venison and fennel sausage served with red pepper polenta for dinner at the Fern House in Kilmacanogue. When Sally Mckenna and the kids had breakfast one morning in Egg, what struck them was how, even at that time of day, there were fresh herbs in the carafe of water, cranberries in the cranberry juice, pieces of apple in the apple juice. The simple things make all the difference, and paying attention to them is what creates the Wow! factor. And Avoca is all about that Wow!, from the moment you enter until you leave. Driving from Belfast to Kilkenny one evening, John McKenna picked up dinner-to-go at Rathcoole. It was, of course, only brilliant.

● **OPEN:** Avoca Mill Store, Avoca Village 9.30am-5.30pm; Mount Usher Gardens 10.30am-5.20pm; Kilmacanogue, Fern House Cafe 9am-5pm Mon-Sat, 9.30am-6pm Sun, late opening Thu-Sat; Sugar Cafe 9am-5pm Mon-Fri, 10am-5pm Sat, 10am-5.30pm Sun; Powerscourt 9.30am-5.30pm Mon-Fri, 10am-6pm weekends; Rathcoole 9.30am-6pm Mon-Sat, 10am-6pm Sun; Suffolk St 10am-6pm, late opening Thur-Sat; Letterfrack 9am-6pm; Moll's Gap 9am-6pm; Belfast 9.30am-6pm. Phone to check opening times if travelling.
● **PRICE:** Lunch €20
● **CREDIT CARDS:** Visa, Mastercard, Laser, Amex
● **NOTES:**
Full wheelchair access in Kilmacanogue & Rathcoole.

BATES RESTAURANT

Marino Monterisi
3 Market Street, Rathdrum
County Wicklow
+ 353 (0) 40-429988
www.batesrestaurant.ie
batesinn@yahoo.ie

Marino Monterisi is a chef who is moving quickly, opening new ventures in Wicklow, and doing so to great acclaim for his sheer professionalism.

Marino Monterisi is a busy man. Having gotten Bates restaurant in Rathdrum up-and-running as one of the best Wicklow destinations, he has turned his hand to Woods restaurant, in Roundwood, and his cooking has already been winning acclaim. The food in Woods, in a pretty room that is part of Byrne's bar, is more conventional-classic European fare – pork belly with mash; lemon sole with beurre noisette; confit duck with lentils – than the Italian-influenced food with which Mr Monterisi made his reputation in Bates.
It is still early days for Woods, but back in Bates, Mr Monterisi has trimmed back the overtly Italian nature of the cooking, and whilst dishes such as aubergine parmigiana with tomato and basil and asparagus risotto and panna cotta are still here, the rest of the menu is more widely focused on European dishes – langoustine on sourdough bread; Clare Island salmon with lemon butter sauce; char-grilled Wexford rib-eye with green peppercorn sauce; rosé veal Holstein with egg, anchovies and capers. The room is lovely, and value is keen.

● **OPEN:** 6.30pm-10pm Mon-Fri (closed Tue); 5.30pm-10pm Sat, 12.30pm-3pm, 6.30pm-9pm Sun
● **PRICE:** Sun Lunch €18.50-€22.50. Dinner €19.50-€40
● **CREDIT CARDS:** Visa, Mastercard, Laser

● **NOTES:**
Wheelchair access. Owners also operate Simply Bates Cafe and The Cartoon Inn. Value menu €19.50-€24.50

● **DIRECTIONS:**
Through the archway beside the Cartoon Inn.

THE CONSERVATORY

Lisa de la Haye
The Old Schoolhouse, Laragh
County Wicklow
+353 (0) 404-45302
lisa@theconservatory.ie
www.theconservatory.ie

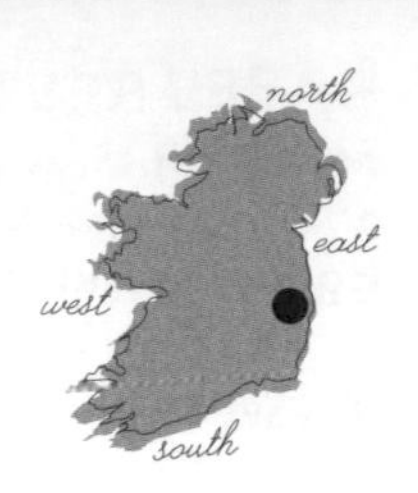

A most romantic setting in leafy Laragh is the perfect, almost poetic location for Lisa de la Haye's aesthetically inspiring restaurant.

Picture an old stone house in leafy Laragh with a fine conservatory on one end filled with visitors taking tea, an Aga in the old French country kitchen beyond storing tea-towels, and unique antique pieces adding the finishing touches to elegant rooms inside, and you have the romantic setting of Lisa de la Haye's restaurant and guesthouse. Whether you want to hire The Conservatory for private dinner parties or drop in for lunch while out for a walk, this place will serve up generous helpings of refined country hospitality and cooking. The menu changes regularly but always offers pleasing, hearty fare. Starters include the likes of prawns tossed in garlic butter, and Cashel Blue and leek tart served with a generous salad, while mains such as beef and Guinness stew, wild venison and beetroot casserole, and pan-fried chicken breast with wild mushrooms and tagliatelle would satisfy a bigger appetite. Pastry chef Leonora bakes an ace selection of breads, cakes and scones, served warm with your choice of jam. The Conservatory is simply a gem.

- **OPEN:** 10am-6pm Wed-Mon (closed Tue), open till 9.30pm Thu-Sat
- **PRICE:** Lunch €10-€20, €40
- **CREDIT CARDS:** Visa, Mastercard, Laser

- **NOTES:**
Wheelchair access.

- **DIRECTIONS:**
From N11drive through Kilmacanogue, turn right into Roundwood, drive through Annamoe and into Laragh where restaurant is on the right before the bridge.

GRANGECON CAFÉ

Richard & Jenny Street
Kilbride Road, Blessington
County Wicklow
+353 (0) 45-857892
grangeconcafe@eircom.net

"Feeding our customers some of the best we can", says Richard Street. That's just what Richard and Jenny have always done: the best they can.

Richard and Jenny Street do things their way, and they don't do things the easy way, and that is why the iconic Grangecon – a seemingly simple daytime place to eat just off the main strip of Blessington – is in this book. "Jenny Street will NOT allow the Grangecon Café to cut corners", says Richard, so when you buy that sausage roll, it's got organic pork meat from Dominic Leonard's farm in Durrow, and that Gubbeen special has their own sweet chilli jam and fresh focaccia bread they bake every morning, and there is organic St Tola goats' cheese in the salad, and the lemonade is made by themselves, and the wines are from Simon Tyrrell who knows all there is to know about the fruit of the vine. Put this determination, this stubbornness, this obsessive care about standards, this devoted creativity and these fabulous foods together, and you have the café from heaven, which is what little Grangecon is. "No margarine to be seen" is what Richard says of his café, and that pithy phrase perfectly encapsulates this brilliant endeavour: no margarine to be seen!

- **OPEN:** 9am-4pm Mon-Sat
- **PRICE:** Lunch €10-€20
- **CREDIT CARDS:** Visa, Mastercard, Laser

● NOTES:
Wheelchair access. Cooked food available to take away.

● DIRECTIONS:
Blessington is on the N81 route south of Dublin to Enniscorthy. Heading south, turn left at the second set of traffic lights in the village: Grangecon is on the left.

THE STRAWBERRY TREE

Evan Doyle
Macreddin Village, Aughrim
County Wicklow
+353 (0) 402-36444
www.brooklodge.com
brooklodge@macreddin.ie

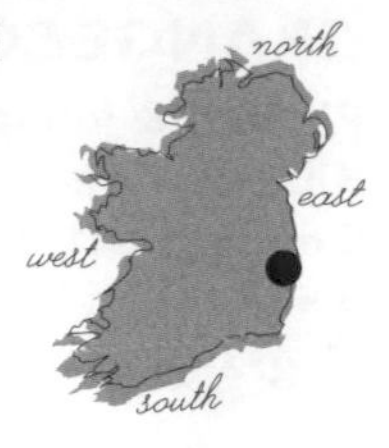

The stunning quality of their wild and organic ingredients means the food in The Brook Lodge can be daringly simple.

The way Evan Doyle runs the restaurants in The Brook Lodge, both the Strawberry Tree restaurant in the hotel and their Italian restaurant, La Taverna Armento, reminds us of a remark made to us by the great Maura Foley of Kenmare, back when we were writing a book called *How to Run a Restaurant*. "In food, simplicity", said Mrs Foley. Maybe Mr Doyle inhaled that same Kerry air – he used to run the original Strawberry Tree in Killarney – but he truly understands simplicity. You might start dinner in the restaurant with their own smoked beef served with wild coltsfoot, then have steamed pollock with beurre blanc. The organic and wild origins of the food means they can dare to be simple, and it's the same in La Taverna Armento, where you begin with a plate of grilled vegetables and cured meats, before enjoying pastas – venison ravioli; spaghetti carbonara – and pizzas with salsiccia and spring onion, or prosciutto and mushroom. Always simple, always beautifully accomplished, and served in two of the most characterful, romantic rooms in the country.

- **OPEN:** 7pm-9.30pm Mon-Sat
- **PRICE:** Dinner €65
- **CREDIT CARDS:** Visa, Mastercard, Laser, Amex

- **NOTES:** Wheelchair access. Macreddin Village encompasses hotel, a market, shop, pub and spa. La Taverna Armento opens from 6.30pm Mon-Sun.

- **DIRECTIONS:**
From Aughrim follow signpost to Macreddin Village. If requested they will send detailed directions: good idea! GPS 52.8796666 -6.3315

Northern Ireland

ALDEN'S

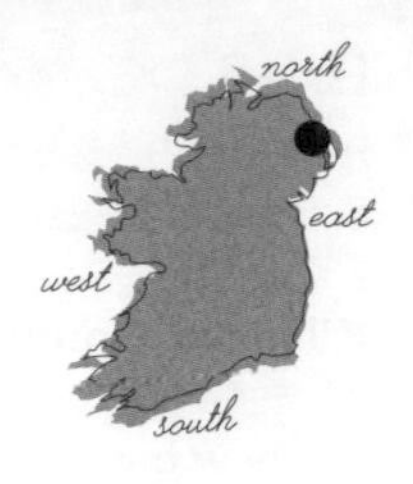

Jonathan Davis
229 Upper Newtownards Road
Belfast, County Antrim
+44 (0) 28-9065 0079
www.aldensrestaurant.com
info@aldensrestaurant.com

Alden's is the classiest destination in Belfast, enshrining all the qualities that make a restaurant into a classic.

Alden's is just a gorgeous space, the epitome of a sophisticated city restaurant, and a place we love returning to. They tweak it a bit – recently they've extended their opening times, and offer a speedier lunch menu, plus they've made it a little more casual – but the character of Alden's will always be urbane and svelte. You feel good eating here, and even a business lunch manages to feel special and not just workaday.

They match the atmosphere with smart cooking, and you get dishes here that can really be described as "very Alden's": roast haunch of rabbit with lentils and salsa verde; rump of lamb with creamed French beans and bacon; mushroom curry with braised rice; sea bass with bubble and squeak. The food is robust, yet refined and serene, and both savoury and sweet dishes partner superbly with the brilliantly chosen wine list. Jonathan Davis was born into the industry, and he has such command of his role as a restaurateur that he makes it look easy – he has that sprezzatura nonchalance, and for sheer value and class there is no-one to beat Alden's.

● **OPEN:** 10am-10pm Mon-Thu, 10am-11pm Fri & Sat, noon-4.30pm Sun
● **PRICE:** Lunch £7.95-£12, Dinner £25-£30
● **CREDIT CARDS:** All major cards accepted

● **NOTES:**
Wheelchair access. Special Dinner menu, £18.50-£22.75 Mon-Thu

● **DIRECTIONS:**
On the Upper Newtownards Road, near the cross roads with Sandown Road.

BALLOO HOUSE

Ronan & Jenny Sweeney
& Danny Millar
1 Comber Road
Killinchy, County Down
+ 44 (0) 28-9754 1210
www.balloohouse.com

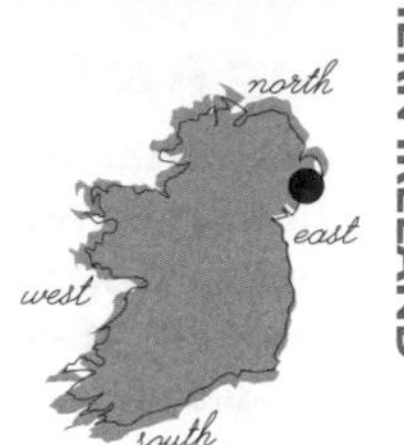

Danny Millar is as distinctive a chef as you will find, with an instinct and temperament for cooking that is his alone.

He brings it all back home, does Danny Millar. He has the home-grown, cutting-edge skills honed by working with great N.I. chefs like Paul Rankin and the late Robbie Millar – you don't get a better c.v. than that – and then he draws in the local foods he can – Lissara duck; Glenarm salmon; Rademon estate pigeon; Strangford prawns; local Dexter beef; Finnebrogue venison. Put those skills and those foods together and you have the magic of Balloo House, where you will find a cuisine of rare balance and purity. Millar's particular gift is to effect unusual pairings, combinations that seem strange until you taste them, when they make perfect, if surprising, sense: Strangford prawn with bak choi; pickled carrots with pigeon; cranberry jus with Lissara duck; sage gnocchi with saddleback pork. The result is somewhere between the richness of classic cuisine and the chutzpah of the post-modern school, but it is very much Danny Millar's own place, and his food is as distinctive to eat as it is distinctive to think. The Sweeneys run the rooms – restaurant and bistro – with quiet élan.

- **OPEN:** 6pm-9pm Tue & Wed, 6pm-9.30pm Thur-Sat, noon-3pm Sun
- **PRICE:** Dinner £35-£40
- **CREDIT CARDS:** All major cards accepted

NOTES:

Bistro food served in the bar noon-9pm Mon-Sun, 'till 8.30pm Sun. Wheelchair access downstairs.

DIRECTIONS:

Follow signs for Killinchy and the restaurant is on the roadside.

THE BAY TREE

Sue & William Farmer
118 High Street, Holywood
County Down, BT18 9HW
+44 (0) 28-9042 1419
www.baytreeholywood.co.uk
info@baytreeholywood.co.uk

Sue and William continue to get better in The Bay Tree, thanks to an artisan ethos, and hard work. These guys make everything from scratch.

There it is on the Bay Tree's web site: "We make *everything* ourselves". Now, that's our sort of restaurant. In an age when every restaurant can buy everything from The Man in the Van, to declare that your ethos is that of the artisan is what we like to hear at Bridgestone Central. Sue and William Farmer are purists, not to mention very, very hard workers, and together they have powered this Holywood icon right to the pinnacle of contemporary Northern Irish cooking. How have they done it? Simplicity in the cooking, actually, and a sense of fun, a joy in putting their spin on familiar dishes, whether its Dexter T-bone served with Kilkeel lobster cocktail and chunky chips, or their signature poulet grand-mere with mash. This sort of riffing puts us in mind of Diana Henry, one of the great N.I. cooks, and their eye for creating dazzling detail is pure Diana – tomato, sultana and fennel relish with lamb shank; blackberry shallots with hake; cherry jus with duck. Beautiful food, great staff, and a collegiate atmosphere that embraces everyone here.

- **OPEN:** 8am-9.30pm Mon-Sat, closed at 5pm on Tue and open 9.30am Sat. 10am-3pm Sun
- **PRICE:** Lunch £10-£15, Dinner £25-£30
- **CREDIT CARDS:** All major cards accepted

- **NOTES:** Limited wheelchair access. Go! Bay Tree open 9am-5.30pm Mon-Fri. Early bird 5.30pm-6.30pm

- **DIRECTIONS:**

Through an archway at the top of Holywood, when heading in the direction of Belfast.
GPS 54.639481 -5.837536

BROWNS

Ian Orr
1 Bonds Hill, Waterside
Derry, County Londonderry
+44 (0) 28-7134 5180

www.brownsrestaurant.com

eat@brownsrestaurant.com

Ian Orr will be one of the superstars of the next generation of chefs, finally putting Derry on the map. Get there early for bragging points.

Ian Orr's restaurant is the first stand-alone restaurant west of the River Bann to have ever made it into the Bridgestone 100 Best Restaurants in Ireland. But that's just the beginning, for we are sure Mr Orr is going to be one of the most celebrated of the new generation of chefs in Ireland. He is a wildly gifted cook, and Browns already has a confidence, an élan, about its style, its service and its cooking that is utterly winning. Eat your way through the menu dishes – Willie Lynch's oysters with hazelnut and coriander butter; Portavogie scallops with O'Doherty's black pudding; Fivemiletown goat's cheese wrapped in Parma with caramelized figs and chestnut honey; 21-day aged Kettyle beef with borlotti beans and Parmesan purée; Lough Erne lamb with red onion and spinach tartlet – and you see at work a chef who enjoys true empathy with his ingredients, a cook who can make these dishes sing. The perfection of the food is complemented by superb service from the brilliant Danielle, and the region west of the Bann has finally gotten lucky in having Ian Orr cooking here.

● **OPEN:** noon-2.30pm, 6pm-11pm Tue-Fri, 6pm-11pm Sat, champagne breakfast Sun 10am-noon, Sun lunch noon-3pm
● **PRICE:** Lunch from £7.95-£23.95, Dinner £25-£30
● **CREDIT CARDS:** Visa, Mastercard, Laser

● **NOTES:**
Full disabled access. Recommended for vegetarians, Theatre dinner £15-£18, 6pm-7.30pm Tue-Fri

● **DIRECTIONS:**
Leave the A2 at Spencer Road in the Waterside district.

GINGER

Simon McCance
68-72 Great Victoria Street
Belfast
County Antrim
+44 (0) 28-9024 4421
www.gingerbistro.com

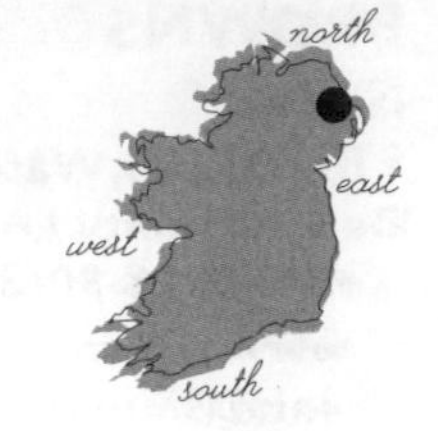

Simon McCance is the man, a funky guy whose soulfulness lights up his cooking and his brilliant bistro.

hot

A friend wrote to us recently, describing a new discovery where, he said "the food tastes as if they really like you". Simon McCance's food tastes like he really likes you, simple as that. How so? Because the flavours and textures he creates are so open, so sweet and moreish, so friendly and unpretentious, so genuine and generous. It's no surprise that he loves the lip-smackin' savoury notes in twice cooked Oriental duck with spiced plum sauce, or that he pairs sweet pickled slaw with Thai salmon cakes, or that he will offer such primal comfort food as a puff pastry pie of spinach and ricotta alongside such tasty specialities. It's all designed to have maximum impact through maximum pleasure, and that's what Ginger is all about: maximum pleasure. So, order up the toasted asparagus with goat's cheese, or the monkfish wrapped in Parma ham with celeriac purée, or the sea bream with Parmentier potatoes, or the soft centre chocolate cake, and get a taste of food that tastes as if the chef really likes you, really, really likes you. Lovable stuff.

- **OPEN:** noon-3pm Tue-Sat, 5pm-9pm Mon, 5pm-9.30pm Tue-Thu, 5pm-10pm Fri & Sat
- **PRICE:** Lunch £15-£20, Dinner £30
- **CREDIT CARDS:** Visa, Mastercard, Maestro

- **NOTES:**

Wheelchair access. Pre-theatre menu, 5pm-7pm Tue-Fri

- **DIRECTIONS:**

200m up the street from the Crown Bar, leading out of the city.

JAMES STREET SOUTH

Niall & Joanne McKenna
21 James Street South
Belfast, County Antrim
+44 (0) 28-9043 4310
www.jamesstreetsouth.co.uk
info@jamesstreetsouth.co.uk

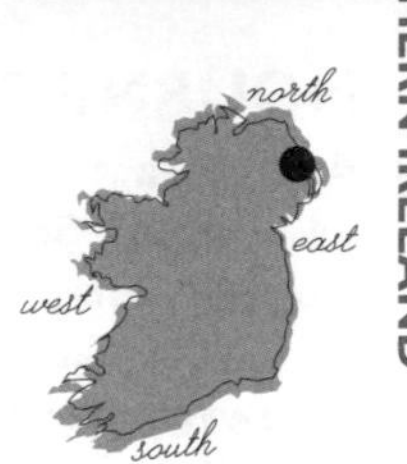

Beautiful room; beautiful food; fantastic service; great value: Niall and Joanne McKenna's restaurant simply has the lot.

"Our favourite room: so white and cool with excellent food". That's how our friend Eugene summed up Niall McKenna's smart, city-centre restaurant, and we wouldn't be able to come up with a better one-liner to describe a restaurant that is appealing in every way – its aesthetic; its service; its cooking. We love the coolness, and the fact that it isn't cold, and that the whiteness isn't bland. And Mr McKenna's food, then, enters this beautiful room like works of art concocted on plates: a museum of contemporary culinary arts. There is vigour in this beautifully realised cooking, and the vigour is married to incredible technique, and impish creativity. It's lush food – McKenna likes lobster, foie gras, turbot and game, but that cool note keeps everything balanced, so the foie gras is counterpointed by apple and rhubarb; lobster has tart, clean radish; turbot has sweet razor clams, pigeon has crisp pear and sherry jus. Irresistible cooking in a sublime room, and the service is, in that inimitable Belfast fashion, as professional, controlled and friendly as the food itself.

- **OPEN:** noon-2.45pm, 5.45pm-10.45pm Mon-Sat; 5.30pm-9pm Sun
- **PRICE:** Lunch £14.50-£16.50, Dinner £23-£35
- **CREDIT CARDS:** All major cards accepted

● NOTES:
Wheelchair access. Pre-theatre menu £16.50 for two courses, £18.50 for three courses.

● DIRECTIONS:
From the City Hall, travel up Bedford Street, and James Street South is the first street on the right.

MOURNE SEAFOOD BAR

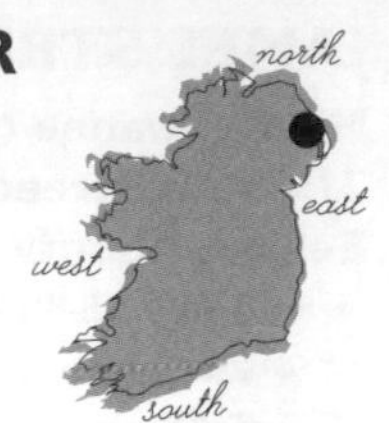

Andy Rea
34-35 Bank Street, Belfast
County Antrim
+ 44 (0) 28-9024 8544
www.mourneseafood.com
belfast@mourneseafood.com

Meet up with the mother and the siblings in the Mourne, and Andy Rea's fab fish cookery makes sure everyone is happy.

So, there is Mrs McKenna and three of her kids – Belinda, Jakki and John – meeting up in the Mourne Seafood Bar for a spot of seafood at lunchtime, and wondering what to have: fillet of shark, Mum? Hm-mmm. What about the hake with wild mushroom risotto cake? Mushrooms wouldn't be her thing now. Belinda is having the prawn risotto with tomato, basil and langoustine butter; John is having the shark with salsa rosso, herb roast potatoes and crunchy fennel salad, Jakki is going to opt for the seabream with saffron new potatoes, spring veg and mussel nage, and Mum will have the beer-battered fish and chips, and we'll have a bottle of Turckheim Pinot Blanc and everything is... well, perfect, actually. Sublime fish cooking, great conversation, laughter, nice wine, sure this is why restaurants exist, so the generations can be brought together by the promise of great cooking. And Andy Rea will never let you down when it comes to great cooking, which makes the Mourne one of the best places for a get-together. A perfect restaurant.

● **OPEN:** noon-5pm Mon, noon-9.30pm Tue-Thur, noon-4pm, 6pm-10.30pm Fri & Sat, 1pm-6pm Sun
● **PRICE:** Lunch £6-£13, Dinner £20-£25
● **CREDIT CARDS:** Visa, Mastercard, Maestro, Amex

● **NOTES:** Wheelchair access. No bookings at lunchtime. Private dining room.

● **DIRECTIONS:**
Just off Royal Avenue, in between Tesco and Primark. Sat Nav 54°35'58.19"N 5°55'56.11"W

NICK'S WAREHOUSE

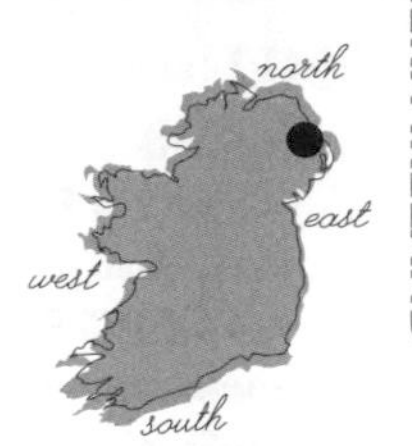

Nick & Kathy Price
35-39 Hill Street
Belfast, County Antrim
+44 (0) 28-9043 9690
www.nickswarehouse.co.uk
info@nickswarehouse.co.uk

Nick Price called his first book *The Accidental Chef*. Nothing accidental about his culinary brilliance, we say.

It is a joy to see that Nick Price has finally gotten around to writing a book about his working life. *The Accidental Chef: The Nick's Warehouse Cookbook* is friendly, funny, and all about families: Mr Price's own family, the family of staff in the Warehouse, the family of customers who have been going there for two decades, and indeed those who have been eating Nick's food ever since Daft Eddie's on Sketrick Island, which we remember from more than thirty years ago: we can still see those tables of sparkling fresh salads, such a revelation, and such a culinary revolution, in Northern Ireland in 1979. What sets Nick Price apart is his sense of humour, and his sense of taste, and he puts both to work everyday in the wonderful Warehouse. But he is also modest, and in his book he disagrees, as we would have expected him to do, with our assessment of his status – we have called Mr Price the most important cook in the history of Northern Ireland. This time, we are right, and he is wrong, but we aren't expecting him to agree with us anytime soon. So, do buy the book.

- **OPEN:** noon-3pm, 6pm-10pm Tue-Sat
- **PRICE:** Lunch £10-£20, Dinner £17.50-£20.50
- **CREDIT CARDS:** All major cards accepted.

● NOTES:
Wheelchair access. Check web for on-line wine.

● DIRECTIONS:
At the rere of St Anne's Cathedral.

SHU

Alan Reid
253 Lisburn Road
Belfast, County Antrim
+44 (0) 28-9038 1655
www.shu-restaurant.com
eat@ shu-restaurant.com

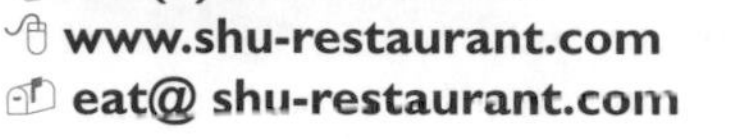

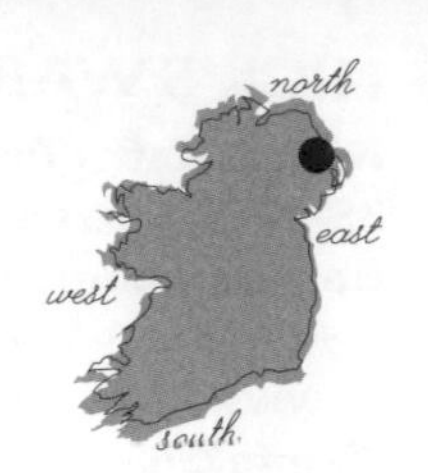

Ten years of success in Shu is easily explained: a happening room, excellent staff, and fab cooking from Brian McCann.

Ten years of doing the good stuff. That's been the story of Alan Reid's SHU, and the good stuff has usually been the great stuff, ever since Brian McCann took up the kitchen reins back in 2004. McCann is one of those chefs with good taste – he has decorum, he has balance, he has restraint, and it means that the voluptuous, rich nature of his food is always controlled, always held slightly in check. Sometimes he will play a dish straight – penne with broccoli, chilli, capers and anchovies is straight out of Ada Boni; corn-fed chicken with creamed potatoes, Swiss chard and roasting juices is straight out of Simon Hopkinson – but we like it when he unhinges the controls a little, like with slow-roasted Glenarm salmon with dilisk emulsion, or foie gras with gizzards (how rare is that!), or when he does another riff with salmon, where he adds raisins, as if in a George Perry-Smith dish, but then subverts it with bak choi. This is artful cooking, full of nerve and confidence, intense and fun, and it's a great atmospheric room with the best Belfast service.

- **OPEN:** noon-2.30pm, 6pm-10pm Mon-Sat
- **PRICE:** Lunch from £12, Dinner £20.50-£33
- **CREDIT CARDS:** All major credit cards accepted

● NOTES:

No wheelchair access. Supper menu, 5.30pm-6.30pm Mon-Fri, two courses £12

● DIRECTIONS:

Straight up the Lisburn Road, across the road from Windsor Avenue.

Index

CONTACT THE BRIDGESTONE GUIDES:

We greatly appreciate receiving reports, e-mails and criticisms from readers, and would like to thank those who have written in the past, whose opinions are of enormous assistance to us when considering which 100 places finally make it into this book.

Our website has two contact forms - one to contact us, and the other to make recommendations.

We love hearing from you.

www.bridgestoneguides.com

twitter

facebook

the companion volume to this guide is:

THE BRIDGESTONE

100BEST

PLACES TO STAY
IN IRELAND 2011

KEEP IN TOUCH WITH THE WORLD OF IRISH FOOD:

Who's Who in Irish Food: read a comprehensive listing at www.bridgestoneguides.com

Follow Bridgestone Guides on
Facebook - we are Bridgestone Guides
Twitter - we are BridgestoneEd

John McKenna blogs at www.bridgestoneguides.com

NOTES

NOTES

NOTES

NOTES